Cricut

5 Books in 1

The Complete Beginner's Guide to Mastering Cricut, with Tips and Tricks to Create Your Profitable Project Ideas. The New Cricut Bible 2022 That You Don't Find in The Box Is Finally Here!

By

Kayla Allen

Table of Contents

BOOK 1:

CRICUT MAKER FOR BEGINNERS

BOOK 2:

CRICUT DESIGN SPACE

BOOK 3:

HOW TO MAKE CRICUT A BUSINESS

BOOK 4:

CRICUT PROJECT IDEAS

BOOK 5:

CRICUT PROJECT IDEAS

BOOK 1:

CRICUT MAKER FOR BEGINNERS

By

Kayla Allen

Introduction

The Cricut machine was created and introduced into the market for a variety of reasons, including to make craftsmen's work easier and to assist others who wish to improve their art and design skills. Cricut was initially considered to have a small use, limited to scrapbooking. Later, because of its modern technologies and equipment, this myth was dispelled; it can do much more than only make scrapbooks; just the imagination can restrict it. People nowadays not only make their thoughts a practice, but they also profit from it.

The Cricut machine is a one-of-a-kind automated cutting machine for home craftsmen that can cut a variety of materials like silk, cloth, vinyl, wood, paper, and several others. This computer gadget also has the ability to cut and carve, engrave, deboss, and perforate. As a result, Cricut can be defined as an automated digital machine that can quickly generate your desired design on the necessary content. You must use your smartphone or other devices to sketch your desired design in the Cricut design room, then import it into the system and order it to execute its work. Cricut design space is software that gives users a forum with a lot of design opportunities so they can create their own designs using the resources in the software toolbar. The consumer must first download and update the design app, which is user-friendly and includes a range of design resources. After that, the consumer can move his or her designs from his or her mind to the designing app, then transfer the concept to the machine and click the run button to get a hardcopy of their imaginary design, thereby turning their vision into fact.

Chapter 1: What is Cricut?

Among the strongest instruments in an art toolkit are Cricut devices. They are used all the time to produce personalized t-shirts, greeting cards, posters, and a number of other crafts. In this chapter, you'll learn what there is to know about the Cricut cutting machines, how they operate, what they can perform and what materials you'll need to get started.

You may even be unsure which one of the 3 Cricut models is suitable for your requirements. Most beginners can start with the Cricut Explore Air 2 – but the Cricut Joy and Cricut Maker are both wonderful devices! Continue reading this book for a comparative study of the Cricut machines so you can make an informed decision on the right Cricut machine for you!

If you're a crafter who wants to do something, this is the book for you.

1.1 What Is A Cricut Machine?

A Cricut is an electrical machine that can cut various materials such as paper, card stock, vinyl, and iron-on transfers into various designs. Both leather and wood can be sliced with specific Cricut machines! Thin wood, leather, silk, and other materials may be sliced with certain Cricut machines. The Cricut can cut almost anything that will otherwise be cut with an X-acto knife or scissors. However, a Cricut can cut with much greater accuracy and speed than can be achieved by hand!

A cutting machine of Cricut can be compared to a home printer. Instead of printing the design on a paper sheet, a Cricut machine cuts the design from a sheet of paper using a thin, movable blade (or other material.)

1.2 Blades For Cricut

As previously said, the Cricut machine will cut over 300 different materials. However, since each substance has its own set of features, the blades used to cut it are often special. Cricut Maker is the most sophisticated machine on the Cricut line. It has the most blades that can be used for its hardware. The great part regarding the Cricut Maker is that as Cricut releases new blades in the future, they will all be compliant with the Cricut Maker. Investing in the Cricut Manufacturer, then, could prove to be a wise choice.

1.3 The Most Successful Cutting Machines

Die-cutter machines and craft plotters are terms used to describe machines like the Cricut. Silhouette Cameo and Brother ScanNCut are two other cutting machine brands.

The Cricut Maker, The Cricut Explore Air 2, and the Cricut Joy are the three models of Cricut machines currently available.

The Cricut Explore Air 2 is the most common and mid-level computer. The Maker is a huge upgrade from the Explore Air 2 in terms of material cutting capabilities. The Joy is the most recent gadget, and it's a smaller, compact model that's simple to set up and operate.

1.4 How Do They Work?

Your dream will become a fact with only a little effort, thanks to all of these features. The blades and tools can be overwhelming to a first-time Cricut Maker user. For others, the prospect of learning and operating modern technologies may be terrifying. But don't be concerned. We've taken care of it.

Any Cricut machine comes with a comprehensive online manual and other sources of various Cricut tools, making them relatively simple to learn how to use. Both the Cricut machines and Design Space are designed to be simple to use, and you don't need a lot of graphic design knowledge to use them (It does, however, assist you in creating your own creations from scratch). In Cricut's Design Room, there's a library of designs and images that you can easily import as a new project. Some are unrestricted, while others can be bought for a small fee.

To begin, use Cricut's design app or software to build a design. Then, using Bluetooth or USB, you submit the specification to the Cricut cutting unit. The template is fed into the Cricut system, which then cuts it out with a thin, precise cutter.

You may use a wireless connection to link a Cricut to your device, make or save designs on your computer, and then send them to your Cricut to cut. Design Space (Windows, MAC, and smart mobile phone) is Cricut's app that helps you to build and import templates to cut with your machine. A tiny blade (rotary cutter, scoring tool or pen) is housed within the Cricut. After you've created a design in Design Space, you can place your preferred material on a 12 inch wide cutting mat, wirelessly transfer your design to your Cricut, and then insert your material into your unit. Your project will start cutting as soon as you click a button.

1.5 Here's how to use a Cricut

1. Begin by placing the cutting material on the sticky cutting pad. (While the Cricut performs the cuts, the cutting pad keeps the material in place.) Place the mat in the unit and turn it on.
2. Next, open Cricut Design Space and choose a design. Send the pattern to your Cricut cutting machine after selecting your content settings.
3. To begin cutting, hit the button on the Cricut machine.
4. Detach the mat from the machine and the product from the mat once the machine has finished cutting.
5. Learning how to use a Cricut by watching videos is a fantastic way to get started. On Cricut's website, you can also find a lot of useful video tutorials.

1.6 Are Cricut machines worth it?

A Cricut machine is a wise purchase if you enjoy crafting, particularly with paper and vinyl. It will make your cut designs look smooth and professional, and once you've mastered it, it will make your crafts go even faster. You can also make money for your Cricut by selling personalized t-shirts, mugs, decals, and other items online or at art fairs.

1.7 From where can you buy these?

Cricuts can be purchased directly from Cricut's website, or you can order the devices and accessories from Amazon. To shop for Cricut, go on Amazon. Cricut machines and accessories are available at craft stores, including Michaels and JOANN.

Chapter 2: What can I make with Cricut?

You will do a lot of interesting things with your Cricut. In certain instances, this is sufficient justification for purchasing a machine. "The minute you need a tool, it's already paying for itself" if you remember this, you will never hesitate to purchase tools.

And if you are purchasing the computer for personal use and have no intention of selling your work, it is a very cost-effective purchase. Anything from cutting shapes and patterns for school assignments to designing personalized presents, cutting vinyl for home decor, and simply wearing leather jewelry! There are many advantages that can save you money in the long run.

It's almost as if you are paying rent to sit at your desk. If you want to make sure, it will really pay for itself. Here are five ways to benefit from your Cricut machine:

2.1 Sell Cut Vinyl

It will only take a few months for you to recoup the cost of your first unit. If you don't have a large site so start an Etsy store for your products. You don't have to make an effort to publicize it. They will just discover it! Consider how much more money you will make if you are promoted a bit more!

Pinterest is a great place to post your Etsy listings because it attracts a lot of traffic. There are guidelines for using Cricut Design Space stock photographs, but you cannot sell them. Basically, market the products you make. Make something that is completely special to you. The customer could choose the words that would be printed on the product.

Another cool vinyl item to market is bumper stickers. People enjoy adorning their vehicles with fandom, geekery, and other nonsense. Make one sticker of each style you're considering, photograph it, and put it on the market. You should make another if there is more demand!

The best part of selling vinyl is how simple it is to ship; most items can be sent in a single package. It's that easy!

2.2 Sell Finished Pieces

The concept is the same as in #1. Here's a perfect way to do it: make projects for your computer. Create two of something interesting you make, such as an art piece, a onesie, wall art, or t-shirt, or jewelry. Make double of everything. One to hold or give as a gift, and the other to sell. This way, programs will continue to pay for themselves.

Put them up for sale on Etsy or other handmade marketplaces. Projects like these watercolor signs are really common right now! (And they don't necessitate anything in the way of inventiveness).

OR

Custom cake toppers are able to be sold. They're totally on board. They're simple to make and cut with the Cricut, and they're small enough to ship for a reasonable price!

2.3 Use Social Media To Sell Custom Jobs!

These days, social media is a massive source of money. If you're selling something, there are plenty of hashtags to use: #forsale #selling #product...just by using these, users will ask about purchasing. There are several Facebook groups and pages dedicated to selling homemade items...just look for them and join. Add the things to the list.

You can also post items on your personal website, such as "I will cut personalized vinyl for someone who is keen, just so you know." This is another way to get a little extra money.

Simply add a photo of a project you've completed, whether it's a vinyl cut or something else, and let people know you'd love to sell it if someone is interested. You'll be pleasantly shocked! Especially during the holiday season. (Get the computer now and start making gifts for the holidays!)

2.4 Make Money By Selling Iron-On Vinyl.

Iron-on is a great deal! It's the same concept as selling vinyl. It's simple to package, and all you have to do is provide instructions about how to use it on the requested stuff. Every month, all of these factors come together to make a significant difference.

You can also market finished iron-on vinyl parts. Get some cheap bulk bags and iron on some nice patterns. Create collections for birthday party favors, summer camps, and other occasions. Everyone adores personalized work, such as monograms and initials.

T-shirts for family gatherings and theme park visits! To make shirts for friends, colleagues, families, and others, simply use Iron-on Vinyl/Heat Transfer Vinyl. Charge for the vinyl as well as the time spent on it. They looked amazing and received a lot of compliments on their outing! You can't sell licensed themed products, so stay away from Harry Potter, Star Wars, Disney, the BBC, and everything else advertised.

2.5 Go To different places To Sell Your Products!

Set up a store! This one isn't always "at home." When you put up a boutique or a booth, you are restricted by the number of customers who will come, and you would hope that they will all want to purchase your pieces. It's possible! The other problem is the setup, booth displays, large quantities of inventory, packaging, and transportation.

2.6 Still, What If I'm Not A Creative Person?

This is an expression mostly heard from people. Here is an advice to them "You are just as creative as your tools." Of course, you won't be crafty if all you have at home are crayons and child coloring books. You'll be shocked by how crafty you get if you have the tools to do fun crafts. Get the unit and the starter kit, and start crafting right away!

Here's the deal: You don't need to be a crafty person to enjoy and use this gadget. It practically takes care of anything for you. Consider the benefits and drawbacks and purchase a Cricut.

Chapter 3: Types of Cricut machines

Cricut machines are currently available in three different models: Cricut Explore Air 2, Cricut Maker, and Cricut Joy (this is the latest model).

You've landed in the right place if you're trying to figure out which Cricut machine is best for you. To support your decision, here's a comparison of Cricut Maker, Cricut Joy, and Cricut Explore Air 2.

What computer you purchase can be determined by the kinds of projects you choose to complete. Cricut's Design Space app is included with all these machines for free.

3.1 Cricut Explore Air 2

This is the machine I'd use for the majority of projects. It's Cricut's most famous gadget, and it'll cut vinyl, cloth, cardstock, and chipboard, among other products, for a broad range of DIY projects. This computer can cut almost 100 materials and has four instruments for cutting, printing, and scoring.

The best-selling Cricut Explore Air 2 cutting machines make DIY simple, interesting, and awesome, with the versatility to cut out a broad selection of craft materials and the accuracy to produce precisely what you need.

For fans of well-known materials

For a reason, it is the best-selling unit! It will cut vinyl, cardstock, iron-on, and backed cotton, among other products.

DIYers who want to work on a mega project

The "most important" distinction between full-size machines and Cricut Joy is size. When you want to cut a material between 4.25 to 12 inches, use the Cricut Explore Air 2 or Cricut Maker.

For quick-thinking creators

You'll enjoy Quick Mode whether you're in a pinch or really want to make use of your time. It allows you to cut and write up to 2 times quicker. When dealing with common materials such as vinyl, cardstock and iron-on, it doubles the tempo. Quick Mode is available on both the Cricut Explore Air 2 and Cricut Maker.

For colorful crafters

The Cricut Explore Air 2 has a broad range of shades, which is one of the favorite things about it, which includes Wild Rose and Flamingo Pearl, as well as Emerald, Peach Kiss, Peacock, and also the Cherry Blossom.

Cricut Explore Air 2 can be the computer for you if you want to convey your imagination by coloring your craft area.

3.2 Cricut Maker

This gadget contains all of the features of the Cricut Explore Air 2, including the ability to cut thicker or more fragile materials, including leather, thin woods, and fabrics and 10X the cutting capacity. With this unit, you can cut nearly 300 materials and use over Dozen tools for cutting, recording, scoring, and other pro-level effects. If you'd like to try more complex tasks and play with a broader variety of materials, this computer is a good choice.

For next-level makers

Cricut Maker gives you more options in terms of equipment, products, and possibilities. Cricut Maker has an expandable toolset that includes denser, thicker materials, the Knife Blade, for unbacked and backed fabric, Rotary Blade, and for debossing, engraving, scoring, and incorporating cosmetic effects, the Quick Swap bunch of tools.

For multi-dimensional DIYers

Cricut Maker is ideal for making structural components for 3D designs, such as templates, furniture, and more, since it can cut heavier, denser materials.

For passionate sewers

If you want to sew or imagine you could sometime, Cricut Maker will assist you with the most complex and time-consuming aspects of the process: cutting and labeling pattern bits. You may also add sewing designs to the site belonging to only you.

For smart quilters

Quilters enjoy Cricut Maker because it allows them to cut out quilt and appliqué bits precisely, so they are able to concentrate on the enjoyable material.

For the stylish and sleek

The streamlined design of the Cricut Maker with a shimmery, shiny finish and is available in five sophisticated colors (Champagne, Rose, Blue, Lilac and Mint).

3.3 Cricut Joy

Cricut Joy, the latest Cricut machine, is a more versatile machine than the other two, making it ideal for simple, daily DIY projects. It will only cut materials up to 5.5 inches high, so you can buy really long materials (up to 20 feet). It can cut and write with two tools and can cut and write over 50 different materials. If you want to save money and make simple projects such as vinyl posters, cards, and tiny iron-on designs, this gadget is suggested.

Cricut Joy, your new DIY best friend

Cricut Joy cuts and writes for you much like full-size Cricut computers. It will cut without a cutting pad, including materials you possibly use at home (construction paper, copy paper, etc.), traditional crafting materials (iron-on, vinyl, Infusible Ink, etc.), and modern Smart Materials. It's the ideal complement to any Cricut machine and a pleasant way to get started with DIY.

For those that like to conserve space and are always on the run

Cricut Joy would blend right in whether you live in a condo, a tiny home, or just enjoy the simplicity of limited spaces. Quite literally. It fits neatly in a cubby, looks nice on a fridge, is simple to store, and sets up quickly.

For extra-long project

Cricut Joy is compact enough to fit in the middle of one hand, but it can cut continuous forms up to 4 inches wide and 4 ft long or create repeated cuts up to 20 feet long, thanks to Smart Materials.

For last-minute makers

It is said that Cricut Joy sets up quickly, which is especially useful when you're pressed for time. It also fits with the latest pre-scored Insert Cards, allowing you to quickly create a personalized card before a wedding, a birthday party, or a baby shower.

In Design Room, you'll also find a slew of new projects designed especially for Cricut Joy that take less than 15 minutes to complete. This little beauty is for you if you're short of time.

For both experienced and inexperienced organizers

Smart Label Paper and Smart Label Vinyl are two of most favorite Smart Materials for Cricut Joy. They make organization easy, enjoyable, and exciting. Cricut Joy writes in any font directly on Smart Label, cuts it into any form you specify, and all you have to do now is peel and stick.

You can already see it: an orderly line of herbs, well-organized pantry cabinets, and clean plastic bins that don't need to be opened to see what's inside.

To compare all Cricut machines, click the picture below.

	Cricut Joy™ Simple & compact	Cricut Explore Air® 2 Our most popular machine	Cricut Maker® The ultimate smart cutting machine
Perfect for	Quick, everyday, fun projects	A wide range of DIY hobbies	Pro-level DIY performance & versatility
Max material width	5.5 in	12 in	12 in
Max material length	20 ft	2 ft	2 ft
Material compatibility	50+ materials	100+ materials	300+ materials
Tools / Capabilities	2 (for cutting & writing)	5+ (for cutting, writing, scoring)	12+ (for cutting, writing, scoring, debossing, engraving & more)
Commercial grade performance			✓
Works with Smart Materials for long, continuous cuts without a cutting mat	✓		
Works with Card Mat for quick custom cards	✓		
Works with home printer to print, then cut out printed image perfectly		✓	✓
Free design app for iOS, Android™, Windows®, and Mac®	✓	✓	✓
Connectivity	Bluetooth®	Bluetooth®, USB	Bluetooth®, USB

Chapter 4: Cricut Installation

The Cricut Maker is available in a variety of bundles, including the Everything Bundle option and the Essential bundle option. The Essential Bundle options come with all you need to get started on a new project. Cricut vinyl, Cricut textured board, and Cricut cardstock is examples of these. Similarly, the Everything Bundle option tools to get you started on new ideas right away. We'll go over all of the standard Cricut Maker features as well as what comes standard with a simple Cricut Maker.

4.1 Unboxing of the Cricut Maker

You have arrived at the most thrilling aspect of your journey. The Unboxing of the Cricut Maker. The Cricut Maker is currently available in 5 different colors:

1. Lilac

2. Rose

3. Blue

4. Champagne

5. Mint

You'll notice the following items when you open your Cricut Maker:

- Cricut Maker machine

- One black fine tip pen

- Instruction Booklet

- 50 free projects in Design Space for practice

- Power adapter

- Materials for a practice project

- USB cable

- Pink Colored Fabric Grip Mat (Standard Size)

- Light Grip Machine Mat (Standard Size)

- Rotary blade with housing

- Trial membership for Design Access (Free)

- Fine point blade with housing

The fine point blade and housing are often already installed in the Cricut Maker. But don't be concerned if you can't seem to find it straight away. To begin, look inside the Cricut Maker. The blade is most likely already in position.

Design Space is available for Windows and Mac computers, as well as iOS and Android devices. The following are the minimum standards that are recommended.

- Mac

- Windows

- Apple iOS

- Google Android

Important: To download and sign in to this program, you must have access to the internet.

To get Design Space for Desktop for your Windows device, follow these steps:

1. Open a tab and browse to design.cricut.com.

2. Click on the Download button. The screen can shift during the download. Per browser would be a little different in this regard. In this case, Google Chrome is used.

3. Double-click the file in the tab or in your Downloads folder when it's finished downloading.

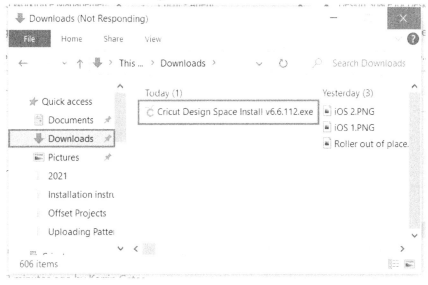

4. Whether a window appears asking if you want to trust the application, click the option to trust it.

5. The installation progress is shown in a setup window.

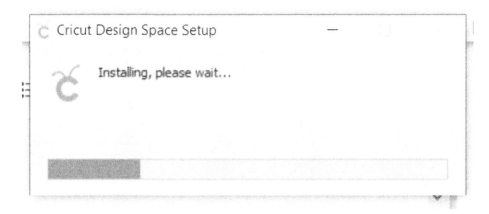

6. Enter your Cricut ID and password to log in.

7. A Design Space for Desktop icon appears on the Desktop automatically. To pin the shortcut to the Taskbar, right-click upon this icon and select Pin to Taskbar, or move the icon to the Taskbar

8. Take pleasure in utilizing Design Space for Desktop!

4.2 Things to know

- The software remembers the sign-in details.

- The software does not auto-save, so you would have to sign in each time you open it because you opted out of the previous session. When you plan, save the tasks regularly and until exiting the

program.

4.3 Procedure for setting up Cricut Maker or Cricut Explore

When you finish the setup, the machine is automatically registered to your account. Follow these measures to set up your Cricut Explore, Explore Air, Explore One, Cricut Maker or Explore Air 2 machine:

- Windows and Macintosh

- Apple iOS/Android

1. Switch on the computer by plugging it in.
2. Use the USB cord to connect the unit to your phone or pair it with Bluetooth.
3. Open the window and go to design.cricut.com/setup.
4. Get Design Space for Desktop and install it.

5. Sign in or generate a Cricut ID, then set up the new machine by following the on-screen directions.

6. When you're asked to take a test cut, you'll realize the configuration is final.

During system initialization, the machine is automatically registered. Reconnect your system, go to design.cricut.com/config or pick New Machine Setup from the Design Space account menu, and obey the on-screen instructions if you did not finish setup when you first linked your machine to your device.

4.4 Attaching Cricut Maker or Cricut Explore to a Bluetooth device

With the Cricut Explore and Cricut Maker computers, you can cut off wirelessly. To connect them with your mobile or machine, follow the measures below:

To sever wirelessly, the Cricut Explore one and/or Cricut Explore need a Bluetooth Adapter that should be wireless.

- iOS
- Android
- Windows
- Mac

1. Make sure your Cricut Maker or Cricut Explore system is turned on and next to your screen (about 10 to 15 feet). Make sure your Bluetooth Adapter (Wireless) is inserted whether you have a Cricut Explore One or simple Cricut Explore.

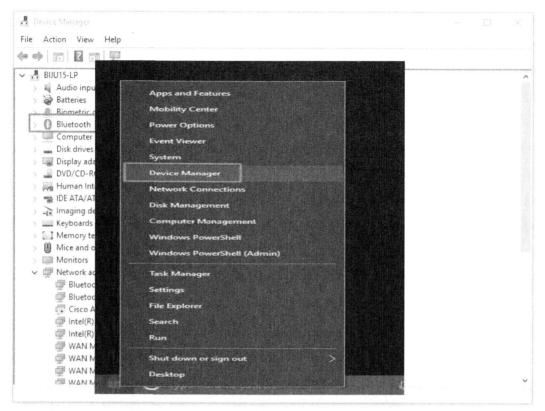

2. Bluetooth is supported by the majority of devices. However, click the right button on the Start icon and tap Device Manager to see if your machine is Bluetooth-enabled.

3. Your device is Bluetooth activated if Bluetooth is identified. If not, you'll need to buy a Bluetooth Dongle, which is a device having a USB port that allows your machine to communicate with other devices containing Bluetooth.

Cambridge Silicone Radio (CSR) Bluetooth Dongles are not compatible with Cricut devices, according to the research. It is recommended to get a Bluetooth dongle that helps audio devices if you need one for your phone. While it is not ensured that all the dongles would work with Cricut devices, those that help audio devices are most of the time effective.

4. Shut down Device Manager.

5. Pick Settings from the Start menu at the bottom of your screen.

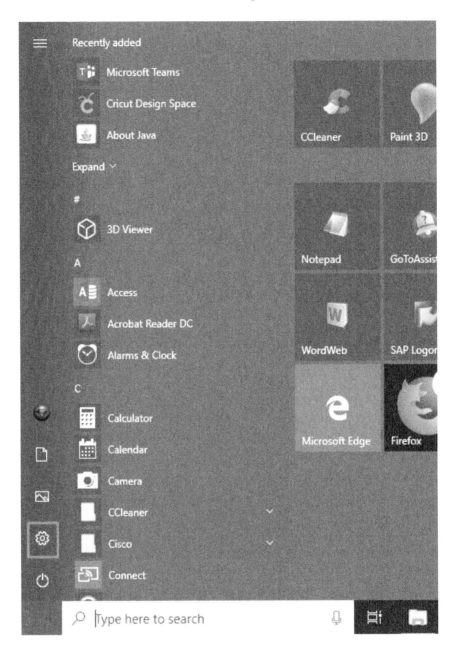

6. Choose Devices from the drop-down menu.

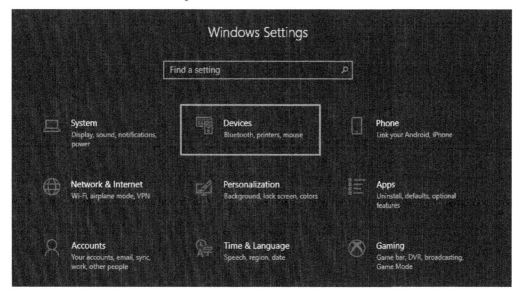

7. Make sure Bluetooth is turned on, and then choose "Add Bluetooth or another device."

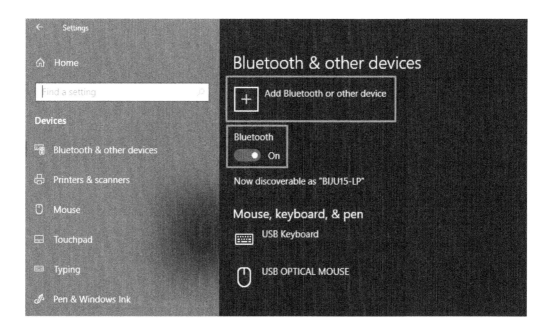

8. Press the Bluetooth button and just wait for a few seconds for the device to recognize the Cricut machine. Choose your computer from the drop-down menu.

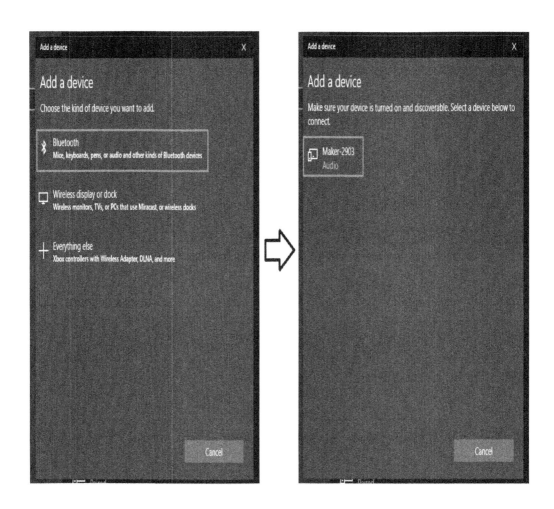

9. If you're asked for a PIN, enter 0000. After that, choose Link.

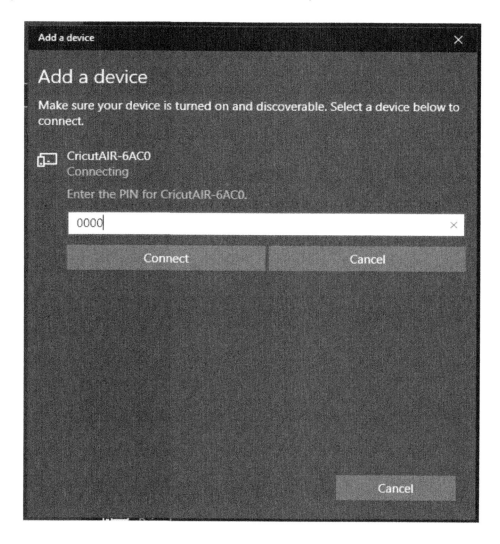

10. Your Cricut Explore or Cricut Maker is now connected to your screen running Windows!

It's common for Cricut Explore or Cricut Maker machines to appear in the list as Audio. If you have several Cricut machines, use the system code to find the one you want to combine. This can be seen on the serial number sticker on the back of the container.

These instructions and screen-shots are only from Windows 10. If you require assistance with a particular Windows operating system, please feel free to contact Member-Care.

4.5 Uninstalling Cricut Design Space

Please take the measures below to delete Design Space from your machine or mobile for troubleshooting purposes or permanently:

- Windows

- iOS

- Mac

- Android

1. Make sure the Design Space for the Desktop is turned off. The program would not uninstall correctly if it is not closed.

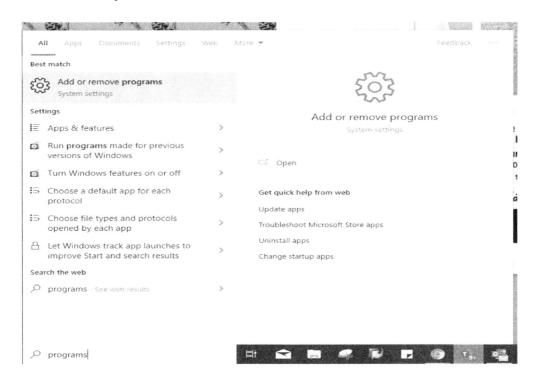

2. Click the Start button in the bottom left-hand corner of the computer and type Programs into the search box. Select the Add or Remove Programs function. The Apps & Features window will appear.

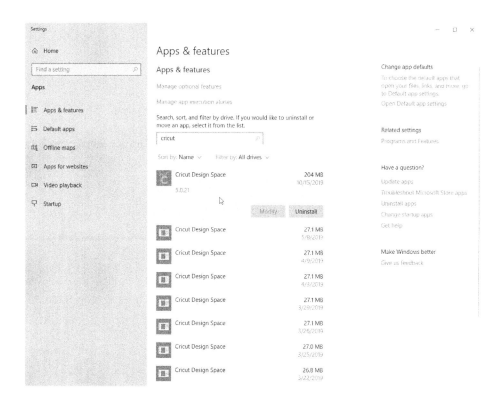

3. Type "Cricut" into the search area. Pick Cricut Design Space from the drop-down menu, then click Uninstall.
4. Verify that you choose to uninstall Cricut Design Room.

5. The uninstallation will be completed by the system. Restart the machine if asked.

Notice that depending on the Windows edition, there might be minor differences. For more details, go to windows.microsoft.com.

Tip: Once you've uninstalled programs from your machine, it's a good idea to restart the computer before reinstalling them.

Chapter 5: Design Space Application

Cricut Design Space is a companion program for the Cricut Maker and Cricut Explore machines that allows you to design and cut wirelessly. Create a startup or visit the Cricut Image Library for thousands of files, predesigned Make It Now projects, and fonts. You can view your projects and photos anytime you're motivated since the software is cloud-based and synced through your devices. To imagine the idea on a real-life backdrop, use the built-in video. Then, using your Cricut Maker or Cricut Explore machine's wireless Link, cut your designs!

5.1 Features

- Build DIY projects with the Cricut Maker and Cricut Explore cutting machines.
- Choose from the Cricut Picture Library's over 50,000 photographs, fonts, and projects— or use your own photos and fonts for free.
- Upload and edit your own photos
- Use fonts and icons downloaded to your computer to design and cut without the need for an Internet link.
- Make home and party decoration, cards and invites, scrapbooking, fashion, jewelry, kids' crafts, and more with simple and simple predesigned Make It Now projects
- Use your device's built-in camera to pose and imagine your designs on a real-life backdrop
- Cut a broad range of fabrics, like paper, acrylic, cardstock, iron-on, fabric, poster board— even tougher materials including leather
- Sign in with your Cricut ID to view your photographs and projects, as well as to make transactions on Cricut.com and in Design Space more convenient.
- Wireless capability via Bluetooth® (wireless Bluetooth adapter may be needed, sold separately).

If your life revolves around crafting and making using the best materials available. Whenever anything fresh is published, you fully try it to fail miserably. The latest Cricut Design Space App is for you. The latest Cricut Design Space App isn't half bad. Really, it's fantastic. You will use the Design Space software to view all of the Make It Now projects and to design your own creations. You can use your iPad to access the entire image library as well as all of the projects you've created on your computer. It's all right there. It's almost magical. The Design Space App would be used by unicorns if they ever wanted to get into crafting.

You can create a quick project now because of the Design Space App. You don't have to take out your laptop or clear a spot at the table for it. You can simply take out your iPad and begin working. You can use the original Explore's Bluetooth connectivity or the Explore Air's wireless technology. You can create and send your project to the computer without any cords in either case. All you have to do now is get up and press the "Cut" button. Suppose the only Cricut could create little crafting elves to do all of the tedious button pressing for us. Instead of elves, Cricut has made it simple to keep track of your project's progress. The app will display notifications on your screen when you are ready to proceed to the next step.

Many Cricut users seem to be concerned about the latest Cricut Design Space download transitioning to the offline web app.

This chapter will assuage your fears. The most frequently asked questions, as well as some troubleshooting tips, are mentioned below to help you make a smoother transfer.

The only thing you can do whether you're feeling overwhelmed or worried about this transition is to prepare yourself. Below are some responses to frequently asked questions.

Why are they going offline now?

Why did the Design Space change? That is the most pressing issue. Why should the software adjust if you are satisfied with it?

Ok, Design Space is fantastic right now online, but Cricut needs to make sure it stays that way for a long time! Moving their site to offline would enable them to improve customer functionality in ways they can't while they're reliant on content changes, web browser updates, and frameworks that might or might not accept the features they choose to implement. Also, auto-update is still an option in Design Space.

Some of you may be very cynical, and many of you are also angry right now. All will be well, and that you will be thankful for the transition in the future. Let's take a peek at a few more often asked questions regarding the latest Cricut Design Space download.

Is the latest offline app available for free?

Absolutely. The Cricut program was always free, and it will remain so in the future.

5.2 How to Install the Cricut Space Design for Desktop?

That's an excellent topic! You should download the web version right now if you haven't already. In just a few minutes, you'll get the app updated by following the instructions.

Instead of using an internet browser, you'll open Design Space on your computer once it's installed. As of January 29, 2020, going to https://www.cricut.com/design can redirect you to the web version.

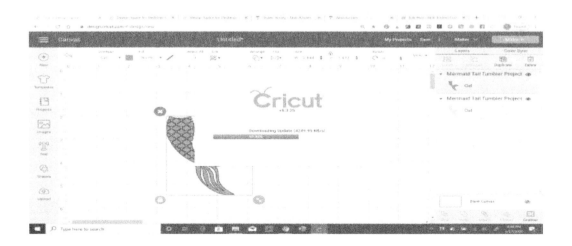

5.3 Which computer is compatible with the Cricut Design Space?

Design Space is compatible with all Mac and Windows operating systems. It is incompatible with Google Chromebooks.

Users with Windows – Ensure that the program is up to date according to Windows 10 so that the latest application can be upgraded and operate smoothly.

Make sure the software is of the latest version, too, if you're a Mac user.

What happens to my application on my iPhone, iPad, or Android phone or tablet?

Absolutely nothing! Most of the Cricut users aren't aware that the mobile version has now gone offline! To put it another way, they're forcing laptop users to use the same apps as handheld mobile users.

What happens to my Cricut Access membership?

Absolutely nothing. Your Cricut subscription, as well as any images you've purchased, will be migrated to the latest software automatically. You don't have to do something – it's as easy as that.

What's the deal with my app being too slow? What's the deal about the app not loading at all?

It's understandable that if anything isn't effective for you, you'll get frustrated. But there is good news: you can get help!

If you're having problems with your program not loading or working slowly, the first you can do is ensure you do have the most recent update of software installed on your Mac or Windows device. This is the issue for 99 percent of citizens, and it is easily fixed.

If you've already upgraded your program and yet experiencing problems, uninstalling and reinstalling the software is suggested until your machine has been updated.

You can also make sure that your hard drive has at least 2GB of free space.

5.4 What if I've done it all?

If you verified all of the things mentioned above, please make contact with Cricut Member Care. They are fantastic at assisting!

They still have a support bubble on the lower left side of the latest web app. This allows you to quickly communicate your problem by choosing a topic, group, and even drawing on the screen to highlight unique issues!

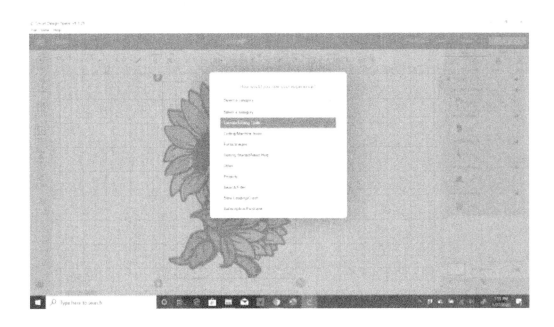

How can I discuss my Design Space projects with others?

In the same manner as before! The sharing alternative is still accessible, but the Link would open in the web app rather than online.

5.5 How can I get Image Files to Use Offline?

Pick a picture and press download in the left-hand corner if you choose to use it while you aren't wired to the internet. You can modify, load and cut the picture without having to use the internet until it has been effectively saved for offline use!

When I open the window, my screen is black.

You can fix this by clearing the cache and reopening the application, according to Cricut.

Design Space is sluggish.

If this happens, Cricut recommends doing a "force-reload." Click View > force-reload to do so.

I'm unable to see any of my tasks or images

If photos seem absent, close the software and reopen it after ensuring that your internet link is operational. The internet is also expected to load photos downloaded from the cloud before they are saved for offline use. Keep in mind to watch this tutorial to learn how to save your creations and photographs for offline use!

For now, that's all there is to the latest Design Space computer experience!

Book 2:

CRICUT DESIGN SPACE

Table of Contents

Introduction

This guide should be accessible and easy to understand to everyone willing to learn. That way, any guesswork will be eliminated, and you can emerge from this experience with a solid foundation in Cricut Design Space.

Cricut is a material design and cutting system specifically known as a die-cutting machine. It allows you to do numerous DIY projects like cards, invitations, vinyl designs, and much more. No matter what creative idea you might have, with the help of Cricut, you can probably do it. Cricut is a die-cutting machine resembling a printer with cutters attached to it. It can be used for printing and cutting of various materials. So, if you wonder what a Cricut machine is, a suitable response is that it is a home die-cutting machine used to create paper and various crafts and arts. It is an excellent cutting machine known as "the perfect entry point to the exact crafting universe." It is an artisan's companion that gives you the freedom to create amazing designs for different occasions. Many people think that these machines just cut paper, but they can do so much more than just that.

If you have never used Cricut Design Space but want to know how you can start your projects and create great designs in no time at all, you have come to the right place. Using the Cricut Design Space, you can do it with all modern Cricut machines. This will show you all you need to know, and finally, it will allow you to make full use of your creativity.

This guide will cover two main parts—The machine and the Design Space Software, respectively. It may seem like too much information at first, but there's no need to get worried; you'll get used to it after a short time and see how all the systems work together. With a little experience, you should be able to use this machine and the Design Space software with ease. In the second part, you will get a more in-depth look at some of the most important features. You will also understand individual interface attributes and how they interact.

What is Cricut Design Space?

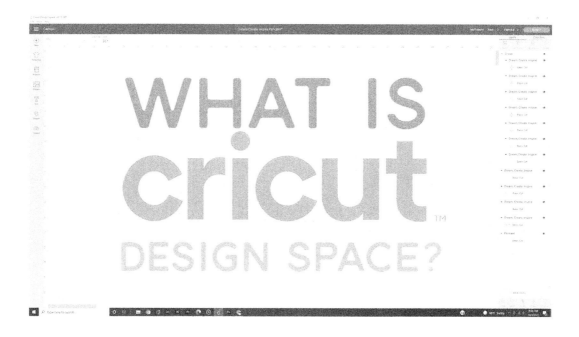

Cricut Design Space is an app used with the Cricut Explore and Cricut Maker machines. Design Space is unique because it lets you wirelessly cut your designs.

You can get Cricut Design Space from the Apple store as a free download.

According to Apple's promo, the app offers you access to Make It Now projects and fonts in the Cricut® Image Library along with thousands of images.

Apple describes Cricut Design Space as an app offering the following features:

- Upload and clean up your images

- Create and cut without the need for an Internet connection by utilizing fonts and pictures that have been downloaded to your device.

- Cut quick and easy predesigned Make It Now projects

- Use the fixed camera on your device to position and visualize your projects on a real-life background

- Create party and home decorations, scrapbooking, cards, invitations, fashion, jewelry, kids' artistries, and others

- Cut an extensive diversity of materials together with vinyl, paper, cardstock, poster board, iron-on, fabric—even thicker supplies such as leather

With these explanations behind us, let's begin taking the steps you'll need to use Cricut Design Space successfully.

The Design Space Application

The Cricut Design Space Application is run entirely from your browser. This plugin will allow you to log in from your computer, and your login information will allow you to download the plugin on any device you select so that you can move from computer to computer with ease! This means that you will need an active internet connection to use it, but downloading that plugin will allow you to leap in and out of the Cricut Design Space as you wish from your device.,

Upon your first login to the Cricut Design Space, you will be prompted to tell the program the type of Cricut machine that you'd wish to install. This may tell the program what kind of machine it will be communicating with to make sure that it's appropriately laying out all of your cuts, lines, and scores. The "New Project" button may be found in the top right-hand corner of the screen once you have finished this step and your computer has correctly detected your device. This is often where you will be prompted to download the installer for the Cricut Design Space plugin that will allow your computer and Cricut Design Space to attach.

Opening the Cricut Design Space Plugin Installer for the first time will prompt you to link your device to the Cricut machine that you have selected. Establishing this connection will allow your computer to communicate seamlessly with your Cricut machine. Once the connection is established between your computer and your machine, you will be able to create projects whenever you'd like without reestablishing that connection. This means that you can import images from other sources, images you have created by yourself, or use any of the various pictures Cricut offers for free through Cricut Design Space or their paid Access subscription.

The first thing you should know about Cricut Access is that you do not have to have a membership to utilize Cricut Design Space if you do not have this subscription. When utilizing Cricut Design Space and all of the capabilities that it has to offer, there is no need to be afraid about being trapped behind a paywall.

Depending on the subscription tier that you choose, the perks that a maker receives as a result of signing up for a Cricut Access membership will differ. At this point, there are three subscription tiers available through the Cricut Access program.

These member perks can make all the difference for the crafter that's avidly creating many projects in a short period. Again, these subscriptions are in no way compulsory for crafters who wish to make use of the Cricut Design Space or its user-friendly interface. Still, these substantial benefits can expect from the membership if you choose to sign up!

Use Cricut Design Space OFFLINE!

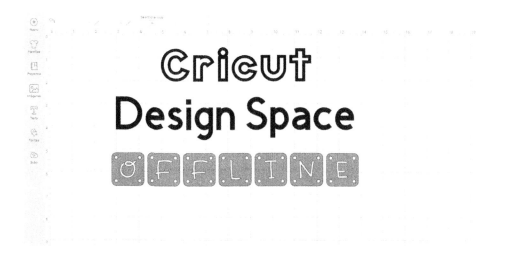

The Design Space affords you great features to shape up, beautify, edit, and organize your designs as a user. You do not only create and upload your custom font and images, but have access to make use of premium images and fonts from Cricut through purchase, Cricut Access Membership, and Cartridges.

Top Panel Cricut Design Space

The Design Space Canvas or interface has a top panel containing design elements for editing and organizing designs on canvas. This panel allows you to choose the type of font to use, make changes to the sizes of objects, assemble and organize designs, and more.

There are two sub-panels under the main panel. With the first sub-panel, you can give a name, save, and make cuts to your projects. The second panel gives you access to controls on the canvas area and editing functions.

Cricut Design Space Top Menu

A tap on this button brings out a whole list of other functions in the form of a menu. This Menu is quite handy. From here, you have access to your profile page and can make changes to your photo. The menu is not limited to this function, as there are other technical abilities it can provide, such as calibrating machine blades, updating your machine's software. Also, you can manage your Cricut Access account and subscription.

Uploading Images to Design Space

Images can be imported from other sources in different formats to the Design Space, where they can be converted to cuttable forms Go to Upload on the design panel at the left of the canvas area.

The Browse option opens the file selector to help you locate the particular image you want to work with. Apart from this option, you can use the drag and drop method to place the file into the upload section.

Different file formats go with different upload flows. For formats like .jpg, .png, .gif, .bmp, the Basic image upload flow is applied, while a selection of. svg or .dxf formats will require the Vector image upload flow.

Spacing of Letters

Designing takes different tactics and methods. One of them is moving letters together when making designs. This option, letter spacing, is applied to reduce space between letters, getting them together. To reduce the spaces, click on the down arrow. In some cases, letters may not be uniform; then, there's a need to, at first, ungroup the letters and move each until they overlap. A combination of the shift key and movement of the mouse will do the job. Hold the shift key down and move each letter using the mouse to make them remain on the same x-axis.

How to Weld, Slice, Flatten, Attach, Group/Ungroup, Delete/Duplicate, Color Sync

The welding tool can easily combine two different shapes to form one whole shape.

To do this, create marks on the layer you want to weld.

Select Weld on the toolbar. The function will be affected.

The Slice tool is ideal for cutting off unnecessary shapes, letters, and other design elements in a project. To access this tool, there must be at least two layers at a time. The first object should be placed on the other, forming your preferred shape to cut out. Mark the formed object and then select Slice.

The Flatten option works in such a way that selected layers can be merged into a single layer. When you wish to print your work, this is quite beneficial. The Flatten tool is located at the right of the toolbar. You are to mark the layers of the design first before clicking Flatten.

Attach have some similarities with grouping option, but with more effect. Select all you want to remain in position for every piece of material, then click on Attach.

Designs can be quite complex, having many layers that sum its whole. The Group tool is useful for such designs. Grouping all layers keep it well organized. When moved around in the canvas area, all layers will be carried along, and nothing will be left off. The layers are first selected to use Group option, then the Group option.

Ungroup does the opposite of the Group option on already selected layers on the canvas. The need to make some changes on the size, font type, or other elements of a layer or design might come up. Select the layer and click on the Ungroup tool located at the toolbar. You will see the effect immediately as the layers are separated.

The Duplicate option makes another copy of a selected layer or design on the canvas.

Delete Removes Elements already Selected

Color Sync is seen as the last option on the toolbar. The colors usually serve as a representation of different materials, in terms of colors. To use a particular color, drag that the color not required and drop it on the preferred color.

How to Start Cricut and What Materials to be Used?

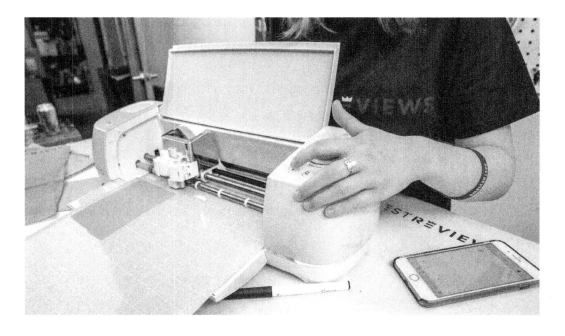

Knowing the Materials to Use with Cricut

The Cricut personal electronic cutter is a truly revolutionary cutting tool that can effortlessly cut any shape or design you can think of. If you're new to the world, suffice it to say that the Cricut is a truly revolutionary cutting tool that can effortlessly cut any shape or design you can imagine. The Cricut personal electronic cutter must be recognizable to anyone interested in home crafts, especially scrapbooking. By the time you've read this guide, you should develop into someone who is much more knowledgeable on what this system (or, more precisely, this variety of machines) can provide you.

The guide intends to deliver an easy five-step procedure you can use to use a Cricut personal electronic cutter to make a visually stunning design. I will flesh out each of the steps with the thought processes you may encounter and the choices you will need to make. After all, you will be able to go off and create something that's currently based on your creativity.

Have an idea

The first stage in developing your masterpiece is to come up with a concept. However, complicated by the technology you're using, it is useless if you don't have any inspiration to start with. It might be that you understand precisely what it is you are trying to make - say, a scrapbook page on your kid's college sports day or possibly a family reunion. You may not be so specific - in case, I urge a quick look on Google for "scrapbooking websites" or something similar. Have a browse through a couple of those websites, and you are likely to find almost endless inspiration extremely fast.

Which Cricut?

It is necessary to choose which Cricut personal electronic cutter will best meet your demands at this point if you do not already own one of these devices. Your choice will probably be based upon your budget and if you will need anything more than fundamental cutting purposes. The precise information about what each version can do and how they are purchased is beyond the scope of this guide, yet this info is publicly accessible online.

Select a cartridge

The following step is to choose an appropriate cartridge from the Cricut options. Again, going into detail concerning the Cricut cartridge procedure is out of scope for this specific post - the very best choice is to go and browse through the numerous accessible cartridges online at Amazon or somewhere similar. You're in a position to buy cartridges with designs and shapes for whatever you might think about. All cartridges are compatible with each Cricut personal electronic cutter variant model.

Customize your cut

With an idea, a system alongside a cartridge setup, you're nearly there. The initial decision-making point would be to choose how you want to customize your design together with the further options available with the Cricut personal electronic cutter. This choice involves the dimensions of this app and works like a page, stretch-to-fit, and lots of different men and women.

Hit a button

In the end, all of your jobs are completed - you should load your paper or card and hit the start button.

Should you abide by those five simple measures, you're in a position to go from a spark of inspiration for your jaw-dropping professional layout in super quick time. I expect you have gotten pleasure in the process and will get the outcome you are looking for!

Tips to Help you Start

Capturing memories on a virtual camera, an HD camera, and a voice recorder makes life more purposeful. Whenever there is a unique moment that you want to grab and maintain a place to return to at any given time, you can accomplish this easily with the advice of these tools. But pictures are still the favorite medium by nearly all individuals. If you'd like to put together those pictures and compile them onto a specific souvenir, you can turn them into scrapbooking.

Scrapbooking is a system of preserving ideas that have been in existence for quite some time, and it has evolved to be actually so much better. Years ago, the creation of one scrapbook was a monumentally crazy job. However, with the introduction of apparatus such as the Cricut cutting machine, things are made much. Great Cricut ideas are available on the marketplace that you might get the most out of. If you are looking to make one, then this bad boy is your instrument.

Scrapbooks are only a few of the many Cricut ideas available on the marketplace. If you know how to maximize it, it can assist you in generating items that go beyond scrapbooking, such as calendars. If you buy a second-hand cartridge, you will discover a lot of layouts uploaded in everyone. These pre-generated themes may be used for many things, such as picture frames and greeting cards.

Only your creativity will limit your advancement using a Cricut device. Along with calendars, you're in a position to layout every month to symbolize the weather, the mood, and special events connected with this. The Cricut machine will allow you to look for ideas; and however, in the event, one cartridge doesn't have the designs you want, you could always go and purchase a different one. It is that easy!

Be a wise buyer. Cricut machines are marginally priced, with the cost starting at $299. That's pretty hefty for anyone to begin with. You may turn to the Internet to find good deals. Purchasing from eBay can likewise be a terrific move but can take many risks if you're not experienced with eBay. In the event you're very concerned about that, you may always wait for a sale to occur at one of the regional cities and buy out there as that's going to have a guarantee, most likely.

Those are simply some of the numerous fantastic Cricut ideas found on the market. Calendars, alongside many other things, can be produced from the usage of this incredible machine. Bear in mind; only your creativity can limit what you can do.

Downloading and Installing Design

Space

You've got a Cricut Explore Air 2 now, and you need to know how to pair your machine with Design Space and the device you usually use to connect to the internet. I have instructions for pairing it with iOS, Android, Windows, and Mac devices. It doesn't matter what device you use, and you will find instructions for it here.

If your Android, iPhone, Mac, or laptop is over five years old, you need to ensure that your device has all the requirements required for installing the software.

Cricut had an online version that didn't require internet at one time. After downloading the App, you can use it offline with your iOS and Desktop device but not an Android device.

There are three steps you have to do when you are connecting and setting up your Cricut, and it doesn't matter which device you have:

- You have to install Design Space

- You have to connect your Explore Air 2 to your device

- You have to pair your Explore Air 2 to your Cricut account

The first two steps will be different for every device since every operating system is different. But, pairing your Explore Air 2 to your Cricut account will be very similar since you will be using the same interface.

Installing Design Space to a Windows Device

Before this process, you need to make sure your Explore Air 2 is on and at least 15 feet away from your device. If you have to use a USB cable, your device will have to be a bit closer.

Installing Design Space on a windows device is very easy. First, you will open your web browser and go to https://design.cricut.com/#/launcher.

You should see "download" on your screen. Click on it and save the software to your device. Once it has been downloaded, you should see it at the bottom of your browser's screen. Click this once the download has finished.

Once the installation process is complete, a new window will appear on your computer screen to display the results. Connecting your Explore Air 2 to your computer is the first step towards getting the most out of your new device.

Connecting Explore Air 2 to A Windows Computer

This process is easy. You have two options:

- You can always connect your Explore Air 2 and your computer with a USB cable without having to do anything else.

- Since the Explore Air 2 is Bluetooth compatible, you could connect them through Bluetooth if your computer is also Bluetooth compatible.

If you want to connect your machine with Bluetooth, go to your "windows settings." If you aren't sure where to find this, go to the search box on your taskbar and begin typing Bluetooth. Once you are in "settings," find "Bluetooth and other devices," then click on it. You need to make sure your Bluetooth has been turned on for this to work.

Find your Explore Air 2. You should notice a little window appear on your screen. Choose "Bluetooth." Keep in mind your machine has to be turned on before it will show up. If you are prompted and required to enter a PIN, enter 0000 and then click "connect" on the screen. Congratulations, you have just paired your Explore Air 2 with your Windows device.

Installing Design Space on a Macbook and Pairing It to Your Cricut

Before you begin this process, turn your Explore Air 2 on and place it 15 feet away from your Macbook. If you have to use a USB cable, they will have to be closer together.

The first thing you have to do is open your web browser and type in https://design.cricut.com/#/launcher. Find and click "download" to get the software saved onto your computer.

Once it has been downloaded onto your Mac, you should see it at the bottom of your browser. Just click on it once the download has finished. If you don't see the file at the bottom of the browser, find and open your "downloads folder." Then, when you've located the file, double-click on it to begin the installation process on your Macbook.

You should see a small window with the Applications icon and Cricut logo on it will open. Click and drag the Cricut logo and drop it in the Applications folder. Once you have dragged and dropped, the Applications folder will open. Find and click on "Cricut Design Space" to launch the software.

If you downloaded the program from Cricut's website, choose "open" from the drop-down menu. You are going to see a warning pop up on your Mac. You should NEVER download Design Space from any other website.

Before you can go any farther, you will need to pair your Macbook and your Explore Air 2. A new window will open and appear, prompting you to complete the setup of your Explore Air 2. As part of the process, it will prompt you to log into Design Space.

Connecting Your Explore Air 2 With Your Macbook

Again this is a very easy process. You have two ways of doing this:

- You can always connect your Explore Air 2 to your Macbook by using a USB cable without having to do anything else.

- Since the Explore Air 2 is Bluetooth capable, if your Macbook is also Bluetooth capable, you could connect them by using Bluetooth.

At the upper right-hand corner of your Macbook, find and click on the Bluetooth icon and then choose "open Bluetooth preferences." You should see a small window open. Check to see that your Bluetooth is on so that your Macbook can locate your Explore Air 2. Make sure your Explore Air 2 is on before you start this process.

Once you see your device show up on your screen, choose it and then click "connect." It might say "pair." If prompted for a PIN, use 0000 and select "Connect."

Congratulations, you have just paired your Explore Air 2 with your Macbook.

Installing Design Space to an iPad or iPhone

Before you begin this process, be sure your Explore Air 2 has been turned on and is 15 feet away from your iPad or iPhone. To get Design Space installed on your iOS device, begin by opening the "Apple Store" then, in the search box, type in "Cricut Design Space." Once this appears in search, click on the cloud icon to get it downloaded onto your phone.

Once the download has finished, click on "open" to launch it. Before you go any farther with setting up the machine, you will have to pair your iPad or iPhone to your Explore Air 2.

Connecting your Explore Air 2 to Your iPad or iPhone

To get your Explore Air 2 paired with your iPad or iPhone, click on "settings" and then choose "Bluetooth." Make sure that your phone's Bluetooth is switched on so that it can communicate with your Explore Air 2 through Bluetooth. Make sure your Explore Air 2 is turned on, too.

You should see the Explore Air 2 show up beneath "My Devices," click on it to get it connected to your phone. If you are prompter and required to enter a PIN, type the number 0000 into the box provided. Now you need to go back to the App to set up your machine.

Installing Design Space to an Android Tablet or Phone

Before you begin downloading and installing, you must ensure that your Explore Air 2 is at least 15 feet away from your computer or other device.

To get Design Space installed on your Android device, begin by opening the "Play Store." Now you will go to the search box and type in "Cricut Design Space." When you see it in the search results, click on "install."

Once the download has finished, click on "open" to launch the app. Before you go to "machine setup," you will have to pair your Explore Air 2 with your Android device.

Connect Explore Air 2 to Your Android Device

To get your Explore Air 2 paired to your Android device, click on "settings" and choose "Device Connection." Turn on the Bluetooth settings for your phone to look for your Explore Air 2. Make sure your Cricut machine is turned on, too.

Your Explore Air 2 should show up beneath "available devices." Just click on it to get it connected to your phone or tablet. If you are prompted to type in a PIN, use 0000. Now go back to the App to get your machine set up.

Setting Up Your Explore Air 2 to Your Cricut Account

After you have installed Design Space and paired it with your device, you will need to log in to begin using your machine. This process is done pretty much the same way for every device. If you are brand new to the Cricut machines, look for and click on "machine setup."

When you see "Cricut set up" on your screen, you will be asked to pick the machine you would like to pair. Your Explore Air 2 should be connected either by Bluetooth or a USB cable by this time.

Fill out all the information the screen asks for to create your Cricut ID. If you already have an account with Cricut, go to "sign in."

You will use this ID to sign in to both your phone app and your desktop version, and you are also using it to log into cricut.com to buy materials, designs, new machines, etc.

When you get to the "Get Connected" window, Cricut will try to help you get your machine connected, but we have already done this process. You should see your machine, showing that it has already been secured. Click on "continue."

You are now ready to test a cut. You do need to do this. The Cricut will urge you to choose an image, and it will guide you through all of the processes necessary to complete this first cut.

If you decide to buy a new machine, later on, you need to click on "view profile" located in the upper left corner. A drop-down option will appear, and you should be able to choose "New Machine Setup" from there. Click this to get your new machine set up.

If you use your phone, you will need to click on your profile picture, and another screen will pop up with options. You need to click on "machine setup" to get a new machine up and going.

That was fairly easy. Now you can begin crafting all you want.

How to Navigate Cricut Design Space?

The first place you should have in mind in the Cricut Design Space is the top panel. The panel allows you to edit and arrange the elements on the canvas area. It is also where you can choose the type of font you would like to use while designing.

You can change sizes, align your designs, and do many more things. The top panel further has two more panels. The first sub-panel allows you to save, name, and finally cut your projects. The other one lets you have control over and edit things on the canvas area.

First Sub-Panel

Sub-panel number one allows you to navigate from the Canvas to your profile, your projects and send your completed works for cutting. Under here, there is the toggle menu, a button you will click for a whole new menu to slide open.

This menu will prove helpful, but it is not quite part of the Canvas - that's why we do not need so much detail. The toggle menu allows you to access your Cricut profile and change your display picture.

Other handy things you can do from this menu include calibrating your machine and updating the firmware, the software of your Cricut. It may also be used to manage your Cricut Access, your account information, and a variety of other things. Make sure to click on every link for you to explore everything the Cricut Design Space has in store.

Projects

All the projects begin with the phrase "Untitled title." The only way you can name a project from the canvas area is by first placing a least one element.

When you select the My Projects, you will be redirected to your library of created projects. This sometimes becomes useful, as you may want to re-cut an already-created work. So there is the essence for you to recreate the same project one time and over.

Then, do not forget the Save option. It will be active once you have placed one element on your canvas. My recommendation, you should save your project on the go. Yes, the software is on the cloud, but you would be sorry you did not save gradually if your browser crashes. As for files, when you have finished uploading and are ready to cut, click on Make it.

Sub-Panel Two

This is one menu that will surely make the most of your time. It is pretty helpful to edit and organize both fonts and images on your Canvas Area.

First off, the sub-panel has the undo and redo option. Except you are the king of first-time perfections or ordinarily a fanatic of no errors, you would agree that everyone makes mistakes when working on a

project.

Even the most professional graphic designers still have to go through a series of iterations before the final draft.

Line Type and Fill

Then, the line type and fill option is the newest addition to the Cricut Design Space Canvas Area. Before this feature, one would have to modify the line type and fill by clicking on the layers panel.

Linetype has a drop-down menu that lets you change the accessory you want to use while working. You use Cut to cut with any of the blades, Draw with pens, and Score for using the rotary wheel or rotary wheel.

The cut is the typical line type that the various elements on your canvas will have, except you have uploaded JPEG or PNG images to it. What else does this mean? Well, when you press MAKE IT, your machine will cut those designs.

The Cut option, once selected, can be changed to fill your elements. This reflects the varying colors of materials you will use when you cut your projects.

Draw

Cricut Design Space allows you to write on your designs - that is where the Draw option comes in. Having assigned this line type, you will be directed to choose from any Cricut Pens you have.

You need particular pens for what you want to achieve unless you can access a third-party adapter.

When you settle down for a design, the work on the canvas area will be outlined alongside the color of the pen you have selected. The Draw tool enables you to write or draw, rather can cut, when you choose to Make It. However, it would be best to keep at the back of your mind that this option does not color your designs.

Score

Now, Score. Compared to the scoring line, which can be found on the left panel of your Cricut's dashboard on the right side, this is a more effective version of the score line.

When assigned to a layer, this attribute will make all the designs appear on the canvas as scored - or dashed. So, when you click Make It, your Cricut will not cut it, score your materials.

If you are unsure about the kinds of material you need, you can go ahead to read more about it. You will require either the scoring stylus or the scoring wheel for such caliber of work. But do recall at a certain point that the wheel only works with the Cricut Maker.

Fill and Print

You can use the filling option majorly to print and pattern your designs. It is only when you have Cut as a line type that it will be activated, though.

On the other hand, No Fill indicates that you will not be doing any printing, and that is fundamentally when you are merely cutting your design out of your materials.

Printing proper is apparently and arguably one of the essential features in the Cricut Design Space.

This is the option with which you print your designs, after which you cut them. This is handy, and it is the one thing that motivated people to get the Cricut machine and space in the first place.

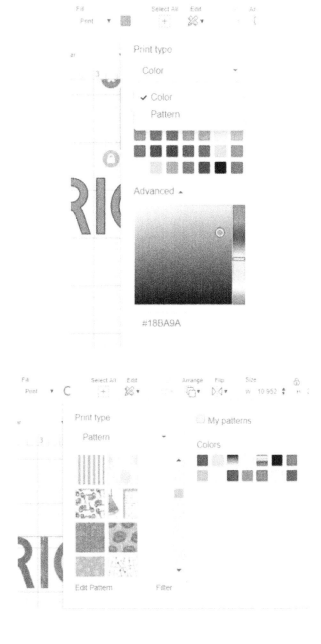

Project Design and Launching the Platform

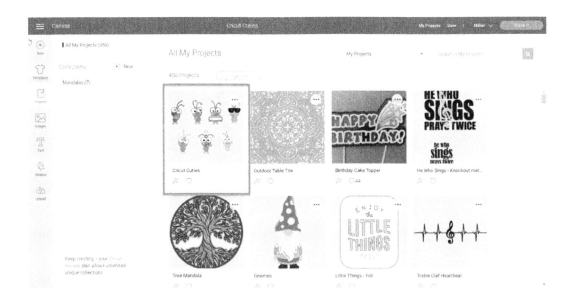

You know the vocabulary and where to locate icons on your canvas. Now, you're ready to design your first project, but where do you begin?

In the beginning, of course! Let me walk you through it.

Starting a New Project – The Basics

When starting a new project, you'll want to know what that project will be and what materials you will be using before doing anything else.

For example, if you want to cut vinyl letters to place on wood, you'll need to know all of your dimensions, so your letters fit evenly and are centered on the wood. You'll need wood that vinyl can adhere to without the risk of peeling. It is also actually very important to ensure that your wood has been properly sanded and polished to your specifications since you do not want any defects.

When dealing with fabric, it's important to understand which inks or vinyls will stick to the fabric's surface before proceeding. You may find even with store-bought wood pieces advertised as ready-to-use, there are tiny imperfections. You don't want any peeling or cracking to happen to your beautiful design.

When working with any fabric, including canvas bags, you'll want to prewash for sizing because shrinkage can cause the design to become distorted after your design has been set.

If you aren't sure exactly what you want to do, have something in mind to avoid wasting a lot of materials by trial and error. The cost of crafting materials can add up, so you'll want to eliminate as much potential waste as possible.

If you're new to Cricut Design Space, start with something simple. You don't really want to go in over your head with this project. That's the worst thing you can do when learning any new craft. There are many used Cricut machines for sale, and while some users sell because they upgraded, others are users who gave up. You invested, and you'll want to get a return on that investment.

Ready to conquer Cricut Design Space?

Before we begin, it's important to note that Cricut has announced some changes to Design Space as of January 2019. "...we moved Linetype (Cut, Draw, Score), Print Then Cut, and color selection from the layers panel to the edit toolbar."

To keep up with any changes, you should often subscribe to the company email list or check the Cricut website.

Let's begin by clicking on "New" from our menu options. It's at the very top of the canvas in the left corner.

An empty canvas will appear. You might have previously started a project, and in that case, the machine will detect it in the queue, and you'll be asked if you want to replace the project. If you don't want to replace it, be sure you save all of your changes, or you might lose them, and you don't want to lose all of your hard work. It's important not to rush so that you don't accidentally delete a project you want to be saved. When you've completed that action, you'll be returned to your new blank canvas.

First, you want to name your project. Use a closely related name so you aren't getting projects confused. If you have many projects and don't use a system to identify them, you might want to consider it.

As you can see from our illustration, everything you need is on the left, under the "new" icon.

You can review different templates by clicking on the templates icon. However, these are only for viewing to get an idea of how your final project will look.

- Here's a brief overview of each icon. They are pretty self-explanatory, but they are worth reviewing for the new Cricut user.

- Projects allow you to access the Make It Now™ platform. There are so many to choose from, and you might find yourself spending a lot of time looking at them all.

- Images are just what it says. This is the icon you need to add an image or images to your project.

- Text is for writing the text if your project has words.

- Shapes allow you to add different shapes such as circles, squares, and hearts.

- Upload your images and begin cutting. This is the final design step!

If you know what your project will be, you can go to the "projects" icon and begin to customize it or start cutting.

We have talked about subscriptions, and it should be noted that you can purchase a one-time design for a nominal fee. You can also purchase designs from Etsy and other craft sites.

When you've done your design, don't forget to save it. You will get the option of "save" or "save as." You will get a message letting you know that your project was successfully saved. "Save as" will save your project as a new one and keep the old one under its name. You will need to rename your project with the saves as a feature.

It'sYour project should automatically save in the cloud, but if it doesn't, you'll have it. It's really easy to get so engrossed in the creative process and eager to see the end product that we forget to press "save." If this happens to you, you'll find out the hard way. It's actually always better to be cautious than sorry in these situations.

Now, you've brought your design to your screen. You want to give it a final look and make certain everything is where you want it. If you're ready to cut, click "Make It."

If your Cricut machine isn't turned on, do it now and have all your materials ready. You'll want to follow the prompts. Set your material and load your tools and mat.

Press the go icon and wait. When the cutting is done, press unloads and carefully remove the mat. Voila! Your project is finished. Wasn't that easy?

Machine Reset

The Cricut machine is like any other machine, which can have problems. You may need to do a hard reset if you can't resolve the problem any other way. When troubleshooting, it's critical to follow the manufacturer's instructions. To do otherwise can damage your machine and void your warranty.

Basic Object Editing

The canvas is provided with an editing toolbar that enables you to make changes to the image as you see fit.

If you make a mistake, it is quite simple to correct. You may utilize the "undo" and "redo" buttons as many times as necessary by clicking them on the appropriate amount of times.

The undo icon will allow you to remove anything from your computer that you don't like. It functions as an eraser, and each click will cancel the operation that was performed before.

Using the redo button will allow you to undo any mistakes you may have made before. Your work will be restored as a result of this.

Another editing tool is the line type dropdown menu, which allows you to choose between a cut, Draw, or score item. The fact that it connects with your computer means that it is aware of the tools you will be employing.

The cut is the default line type you'll use unless you've uploaded a JPEG or PNG image. Those designs will be cut when you click on the "make it" icon.

Use Draw if you want to write on your design. You'll be prompted to select a pen, and you'll use this to write or draw.

Tip: This option won't color your designs.

Your design may be scored or dashed by making use of the scoring tool.

The edit icon allows you to cut, copy, and paste directly from the canvas to your clipboard. It operates via the use of a dropdown menu, and you access it by choosing the items you want to alter from your canvas..

In addition, the application has an align tool that allows you to move your design around on the canvas. If you've ever worked with a design application before, you should have no trouble with this. It may be difficult if you haven't done it before.

The alignment tool's features and capabilities

The functions listed below may be used to move your design around on the canvas. Until you're familiar with them, you may want to experiment with them first.

Align enables you to align your designs by choosing two or more objects on your canvas and pressing the Align button on your keyboard.

Align Left will reposition everything to the left of the screen.

Center Horizontal will align text and graphics horizontally and center them in the document. Everything is brought to the front as a result of this.

Align Right will reposition everything to the right of the screen.

When you click on Align Top, the designs you've selected will be moved to the top of the canvas.

Center Your options will be aligned vertically if you choose Vertically.

Align Bottom will move all of your choices to the bottom of the page.

Everything will be brought to the center by the Center, both vertically and horizontally. You may also distribute in both vertical and horizontal directions.

This will allow you to provide some breathing room between your design pieces.

Additionally, you may flip, arrange, rotate, and scale your design. These options are convenient, and after you've mastered them, you'll be able to swiftly customize your design to your liking.

Conclusion

It's been quite an exciting journey, and here we are. Although this book has given you a lot of information on working better on the Design Space, don't forget to start small. Even if you have so many crazy ideas running through your head right now, you should start with small projects to practice and get used to the platform. This doesn't mean you should limit yourself. Just ensure you build yourself to professionalism steadily.

I can proudly say to you right now that you are not a beginner anymore! You have almost all the information and knowledge at your fingertips, and no one's taking that away from you. However, it would be best if you practice consistently. A little break and you might forget what's important. You might get a bit frustrated at some points while practicing, but that doesn't mean you should stop trying. Cricut is offering you much more than it's demanding.

So, this is the end of the road. If you have mastered all the tips and techniques provided in this book, then congratulations! To ensure you get better faster, you can hang on to this book to handle things yourself. Even after mastering the content, you should keep it close for reference purposes.

Book 3:

HOW TO MAKE CRICUT A BUSINESS

Table of Contents

Introduction

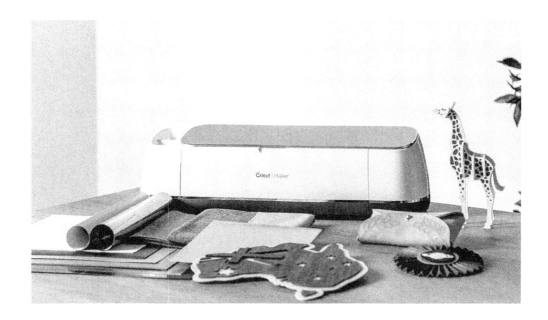

Far too often, highly creative people jump into a business before thinking about the business end of the situation. If you are using a Cricut Maker often and people give you tons of feedback about your crafts and gifts, it might signal that you should go into business with your Cricut Maker. Hundreds of users are doing just that. But what can make you unique and keep you in business for a much longer time?

1. Make a list. There may be one apparent reason, or there could be 3 or 4, but regardless of how many reasons, define why you want to be in business.

2. You might want to be at home with the kids. Have you ever tried to work at home with kids around? Or, perhaps you are making quite a bit with your Cricut Maker already and have so many orders you cannot keep up on evenings and weekends.

3. Working outside the home is not your thing. You have always wanted to be in business for yourself. You enjoy marketing. You think you can take this Cricut business to the top! You have a marketing degree, and you are champing at the bit to be your boss and use that degree to market your projects.

4. Finally, crafting with your Cricut maker feeds your soul. Instead, there isn't anything else you would do with your life for a job. You can work on projects almost 24/7, and it doesn't bother you. Even when you are not working, you are thinking of projects you could do if you were working. This is your passion. You have discovered a technique to make the world a brighter and more pleasant place to live.

5. Make sure you are self-motivated. To be in business, any business, you have to be self-motivated. You may be highly creative using your Cricut, but if you are not motivated to network and get customers consistently, that will be a problem in the long run. Also, you might have to work on projects when you don't feel like working because people need their purchases. Are you motivated enough to keep up the pace a business sometimes throws your way? Also, are you ready to deal with "that" customer? We are talking about a customer who is never happy. You need a plan for the bad penny that will not go away.

Make sure your finances are in order. And then consult with an advisor and an accountant before going into business and take their advice. According to the financial advisors, make sure that you can weather any storms that come along because of low tides in the business world. You don't want to ruin your love for your Cricut by ending up in financial trouble because you were not financially prepared to go into business in the first place. There is truly nothing worse than thinking you have found your dream and ending up in a daytime nightmare.

It's a good idea to ask yourself, "How am I going to get clients?" Etsy? Pinterest? Word of Mouth? Will you market on Facebook? What marketing technique would you use in order to attract customers? Are you planning to go to craft fairs? Think about your options and what marketing is going to cost. Are you ready to beat the pavement? Go to schools, churches, hit up the minor leagues, and everyone and anyone who needs something done by a Cricut?

Everyone who goes into business should have a solid business plan. A business plan is a road map of where you are and going. How many things might potentially cost and the potential income? With a Cricut Maker, you don't have as many outside variables, and most of the success depends on your hard work and persistence. However, you will still need a business strategy, and a solid one at that! Let's get started!

Chapter 1. Is the Market too Full?

Like any start-up business, initial questions need to be addressed to overcome possible difficulties. For example, addressing issues like defining my clientele, the products that might be of interest, where to find them and how to make a profit margin of my sales are important to tackle from the start. In other words, you will need a good and well-defined business strategy to start with.

Choosing Your Clientele

You can target two avenues to sell your products: either by looking at how you can approach the market locally or online. It is advisable to concentrate efforts on one approach to start with as your target is to generate profits as soon as possible. Never forget that your goal is to grow benefit and reinvest it so that your business expands. The quicker you increase your sales, the more likely you will reinvest in new tools or new products, making, in turn, a stronger financial turnover. Understanding your marketing strategy is key to your success.

Targeting Online Markets

If you are adept at higher technical knowledge, you can generate significant benefits by providing quality custom work, bulk offering, or information network. To begin, it is recommended that you focus your efforts on a single technique alone. If you choose, for example, a custom work approach, you increase the chances of finding potential customers looking for your products as they turn to a search engine like Google to find what they are looking for. Websites like Amazon Handmade or Etsy provide a good platform to allow custom design services. Equally efficient is the launch of your site. This strategy is worth looking at. Selling online comes with advantages such as low startup costs and access to the global market with millions of potential customers.

Furthermore, online custom prices tend to be lower than those on the local market. However, access to the global market means stiff competition, pushing products to be competitively priced. Selling online requires certain knowledge in logistics as far as shipping and packing your products are concerned, a cost factor that needs to be considered in your pricing.

If an online retail business approach is more what you may be inclined to do, this approach will give you the ability to determine the demand for the designs you offer and plan the production accordingly. But selling online means challenging the existing competition!

Finally, suppose you prefer to sell your products online through an information network. In that case, you become an authority in the field, creating the opportunity to generate profit with your Cricut designs. By offering blogs on technical know-how or inspiration work, you become selective on the posts you want to take on.

Starting a new business requires a business strategy, the foundation for your future success. Ask yourself who your potential customers would be, what kind of products you can sell them, and the first steps of a future startup business.

Chapter 2. Becoming a Cricut Affiliate

Cricut is a journey where one makes a craft that generates a lot of money, and the sky is the limit. Well, competition is a lot, and the market is saturated, but you can still make a lot of money out of it if you stay true to your craft and do not copy other people's craft. Being creative and different is what matters. Thorough practice shall make you perfect.

Cricut is not suited for all, but everyone can make something out of it as a hobby. Many people use Cricut for their homemade items, decorative ornaments, interior furniture, customized T-shirts, handcraft towels, and much more. With the help of Cricut and the projects that this bundle provides, you can touch the pinnacle of crafting skills. This bundle provides you with every nuance skill and, with it, the projects that shall assist you through your journey to become the greatest crafter around you.

The bundle starts with describing the most basics of the Cricut machine and how to use it. With that comes the nuance description about using the Cricut Software, the Design Space. Having good expertise in the Design Space, one can create almost everything the crafting world offers since the bundle takes you from the most beginner projects to the intermediate level and then the most advanced level. Every project elaborates steps and procedures with illustrative guiding pictures and snapshots. One can say that the author has done justice to its readers.

Tips for Making Money and Setting Cricut Business

1. Attempt to be Diverse

Truly be unique. Carry to the plate, your theatricality, and your imagination.

I'm sure you'd agree with the standout title tiles if you've been in Cricut's designs for any time duration. They became a mad success, and then they were all marketing them.

In the crafting universe, that's how it works. But you may be one of the first individuals to get on a wave pattern trip once the next hot sale comes along. And if you're not patient, the process of handling Cricut crafts may get tiresome and pricey.

Remember that I'm not asking you to innovate the chair, introduce a theme and flourish to your own.

Have a look at the following graphic. It's from two tiles with names I find on Etsy. The one in the topmost layer appears exactly like the other 153 on Etsy for purchase.

Update your crafts at Cricut and put your emphasis on growing profitability patterns. The dealer on edge added her twist on items. What more sticks out? Is the vendor willing to demand more to gain a larger profit?

Don't be frightened of changing formats, either. And when the craft appears like someone else's, the truth is, it's only going to become a trade battle. Nobody's winning.

So when someone else is zigging, you zag. Had this one?

2. *Continue refining it*

This year, I was among the organizer of a festival. A few of my founder planners revealed a girl in a shirt and created personalized shirts. Both of them realize I've got a Cricut. I'm willing to produce clothes. I'd only charge the amount if so.

Yet her attention went right to the girl in her dress. About why? Since the shirt girl creates only shirts because she does them well.

By the way, I'm creating illuminated signs and decals. So they think about me anytime someone needs one of those. I know somebody else who produces earrings. And we also have someone that produces paper roses.

You will think that producing and selling something under the sun would give you more choice, hence more clients, hence more income. That's not the way it operates, though.

More prices, more exhaustion, and more non-selling goods are what it would offer you.

Do not aspire to be the design world's Walmart; strive to be a professional, and the greatest of your region of inventiveness is available. So take a moment to determine what you will be remembered for.

3. *Be Immune*

Work regularly on your Cricut design project. Ideally, each day you can be focusing on it. Any of you might only choose to offer it as a passion and might only be willing to work once a week on it.

Do so as frequently as you can, whatever the routine is. If you neglect your company for days or weeks on end, you're hardly going to get far.

Be compliant with prices and also with consistency. Your clients need to know

what to demand from you. If they feel they can rely on you, they can suggest you to everyone else again and again.

4. Wins Persistent

Look, I don't want to be a party pooper here, but occasionally running a company will suck. And if you try to transform this thing into a company, you're going to have days where you want to leave. There are bound to be days where clients piss you off. There'll be days where nothing functions properly. You're busting your ass and easily going nowhere.

I am taking a deep breath. As I mentioned, this isn't a simple scheme to get wealthy—the citizens who were incompetent left long before. And those people who are good never give up. They might have weaknesses. But that's not preventing them. Be courageous when you make your Cricut currency; never abandon it.

5. How many do you want?

I can't even imagine how much this happens. Somebody buys me decals so that she can produce and sell sparkling tumblers. That's not an amazing aspect.

I asked her lightly how much she was asking for a tumbler since my spouse dislikes shimmer, lol. However, the beads make fantastic presents. She said her price to me anyway, and I shouted, man, that's cheap.

And she said yes, I hope I don't lose capital,

Sorry about what? Do you expect that you won't risk money? Oh boy.

You must know the expense. That's not ideal if you're offering anything for $20 because it costs you $22 in materials! Not at all healthy.

I realize certain items like shimmer and adhesive might be challenging to quantify in this situation. When you hit the edge of the glitter

container, you don't realize how many bottles one glitter container can hold. (Keep records, by the way, for each tumbler you make, take a pencil and place a pass tag on the shimmer container)

It would be best if you guestimated, though. If it looks like you've used about 1/4 of the container and it costs $10 for the product, take ten and multiply it by four and you have a $1.99 glitter cost per tumbler per glitter color. So a $6 glitter premium is two shades of glitter.

Have all of your materials and measure up the costs for the interest in all things resourceful. I typically tack on a $0.5 or two for the expensive products I need when I get all the large products loaded together, but using only a tiny sum is not worth finding together. An example of that is adhesive.

You'll be well able to market the goods for sale until you have the expense of materials. If you enjoy working for minimum wage, don't overlook the time it would take you to build the piece.

The purchase price should be between two and four times the rate of production, according to a decent rule of thumb. Don't fear because people are giggling at you that it's too much. You're the initial, you've narrowed the scope down, and you're a professional, and you're the greatest at what you're doing. And, (more on that quickly) you are utilizing premium goods. People would pay for it happily. Paying for crafts cash.

6. Learn Fresh Daily Anything

Do not be ashamed of knowing about others before you have left. You don't have to find out all by yourself.

Everyone has already done it if you want to learn how to ascend the Etsy ranks or build a good Facebook community, and now they share all the tips and tricks

they know.

At least you'll be doing more selling than crafts at the start of your Cricut Company, making it a priority to discover something fresh that applies to your company every day.

7. Regulation of Consistency

Market-priced merchandise. Any day of the week, consistency dominates over quantities. Let's have a peek at these two custom baskets below for Easter.

Comparing the Cricut with two customized Easter baskets while making money

Therefore the two containers mostly on the right come from the Tree of the Dollar. Everybody and their buddy sold these at Easter, which kept revenues down.

We realize the bucket cost is $1.00, and we say the cost of the vinyl and transition paper is $1.00, which makes us $2.00. They're fast to make, so they're not that terrible. I've seen them for $5.00 each for sale, ensuring we earn a profit of $3.00 per barrel.

The buckets are possibly overlooked or trashed because they were poorly made and inexpensive. Easter comes and goes.

Easter buckets are on the left now. They are cotton, and they are certainly of higher quality. They stick out, and if other crafters are selling them, not all are. You are studying each day, and you realize that these bundles will be used long beyond Easter if we only placed the label on them and we sell them as such.

For the blank basket, we charged $8.00, and for the heat transfer vinyl, $1.00, with a combined cost of $9.00. We market them for $25.00, making us $16.00 in profit for each offer.

That means there's fewer we can offer and raise more revenue. For every one

we sell to earn the same amount, the crafter selling Dollar Store baskets has to make and sell six baskets.

Within a second, let that sink. Less job ensures more personal time or enjoyable or learning time.

People will pay for service and suggest you to their mates for service. The most quality you can do is word of mouth communication.

Chapter 3. How to Make Money from Cricut

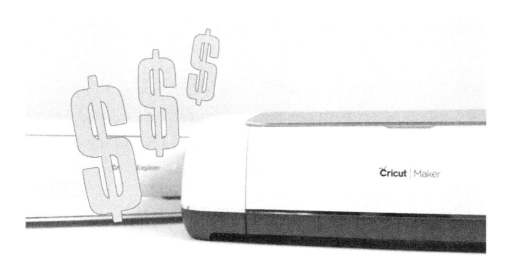

It will be helpful if you can be making a part-time income from what you like doing. You can be having fun with your design and yet be making money from it. There are many people already making money from their designs. You can turn this into a great business that will give you so much money within a month and take care of all your family expenses. If you have Cricut at home and you are not maximizing the use and have time, this section should help you.

How to Turn Your Designs to Money

So many people ask these questions; "How do I make money using my Cricut? Should I buy a Cricut? Is the market too full? Can I still make money? How do I start"? Sometimes it is hard to give a satisfactory answer to all of them because some of the people using Cricut do not want to tell anybody how to make money from this craft. They are averse to disclosing their identities. This book, though, is here to give you all the inside information you need to know if you're going to make money with a Cricut.

When many people start and venturing into a craft, maybe they have a Cricut, another vinyl cutting machine, or perhaps they do not have one, and they want to get one. They have all kinds of questions about getting started, and it is overwhelming at first. It can be confusing and complicated as well, therefore sometimes, you will reach out to those who have one, but they do not want to share their secrets; maybe they are afraid that you become their competitor. But the truth is that everyone can succeed if we build each other up! There is space in the market for all of us to succeed. To begin, let's look at the first of the three questions.

Let us see how we can make money from all the knowledge we have. Someone said, "If you cannot make money from the knowledge you have got, or if you have the knowledge, and it is not useful to you in any way, then the knowledge is useless to you and the society." In order not this knowledge to be useless to you, I will show you how to make money. It is not that your understanding is worthless because you are not making money from it; if the designs created are for your family and friends, they are worth it!

Can you still make money with a Cricut? Many of us are on Facebook, we go to "Marketplace," you may have visited, and seen at Etsy so many shops selling signs, shirts, things we love to buy. The simple answer to the question: yes, you can, and it is not that hard! Even if everyone is specializing in design, and they are doing it better and better, the market can never be saturated. For instance, someone might major only in making T-shirts, another one is making cups, others getting into woodwork design, and many more, even though you will find out that many people are good at in a specific area. So, the market can never get filled.

Now that you are ready, you have got your Cricut, and you are wondering, "Where do I start?" The most accessible place to start is literally by making things for your buddies and siblings. Aside from food, there are a variety of other items you may create for your friends that they would like and thank you for. For example, you can create stickers, design their name, or a meaningful phrase to be printed on their T-shirts, etc. You can brainstorm some things you think your friends will like and start designing them. You can also make a creative design for your children and your spouse. When you are done, you can post them on Facebook to meet people who want you to do the same design for them. This is the easiest way to start without investing so much money.

Selling the Craft You Have Made with Cricut

As previously said, there are several things that you can begin creating for yourself as well as selling to your friends and neighbors; you do not need to persuade them to purchase many of these items since I am certain that they will appreciate your ability to create custom designs for them. So, you have to find out what your buddies like and make such creative designs. For example, if you have a buddy who enjoys football and who owns a team, you might create a sticker with the squad's emblem and write something positive about the club.If you also have someone who sees clothes and you like what they do, you can make a lovely design with its name. You can also make a business logo sticker to put on every dress they see.

You can also make money with your design to look for people who want you to iron on their clothes for them. There are many people out there looking for someone who designs their clothes for them. Look for those who sell a boutique and sell your design to them. This is how this is done. You can offer a free design for someone who sells plenty of plain T-shirts to show what you do; if they like your creations, you can make a deal of how much your design is worth on each cloth for such a person. So, look for local sellers around you who you think might need your design.

Another effortless way you can make money is by selling to groups. You can walk up to a group of people who wear a uniform, have a group name, and ask for you to design for their group. This is easy to get because each group member may like to be identified as a group member and may pay you for your work. Examples of these groups are clubs, choirs, associations of friends, etc. The most effective approach to do this is to first provide the group leader with a free design.

The concept behind this is that if you can persuade the group leader with your design, you will be able to swiftly sell your work to every member of the group; the members may see the design on the leader and will most likely ask him where he obtained the design for his group. Some may even suggest that the group leader get the design for everyone; then, he will be encouraged to ask you to design for every team member. Get the leader interested, and you will get into the group quickly.

Another excellent way for you to sell your design is online. You can create a website, sell whatever you design through the internet, or sell through e-commerce sites like Amazon. Almost everyone is online these days, so you will not find it challenging to sell your designs if there are excellent and attractive.

Chapter 4. Where I Can Sell Your Craft

In business, it is a well-known reality that in order to produce money, one must first invest money in order to generate income. Therefore, if you already possess a "Cricut" cutting machine, you may go to the following paragraph; but, if you are considering whether or not it is worthwhile to invest in one, continue reading this part.

As mentioned earlier, "Cricut" has a range of cutting machines with distinctive capabilities offered at a varying price range. This year's models are priced at $249.99 for the "Cricut Explore Air 2" and $399.99 for the "Cricut Maker" (however the earlier "Cricut Explore Air" model may still be available for purchase on Amazon at a cheaper price). Now, if you were to buy any of these machines during a holiday sale with a bundle deal that comes with a variety of tools, accessories, and materials for a practice project as well as free trial membership to "Cricut Access," you would already be saving enough to justify the purchase for your usage.

The cherry on top would be using this investment to make more money. You can always get additional supplies in a bundle deal or from your local stores at a much lower price. All in all, those upfront costs can easily be justified with the expenses you budget for school projects that require you to cut letters and shapes, create personalized gifts for your loved ones, or decorate your home with customized decals, and of course, your jewelry creations.

These are only a handful of the reasons to buy a "Cricut" machine for your personal use. Let's start scraping the mountain of "Cricut," created wealth to help you get rich while enjoying your work!

At this stage, let's assume that you have bought a "Cricut" cutting machine and have enough practice with the beginner-friendly projects described earlier in this book. You now have the information and equipment required to begin generating money from your "Cricut" machine, so let's get started on you finding out how to put it all together and make it work. The ways listed below have been tried and tested as successful money-making strategies that you can implement with no hesitations.

Local Market

Suppose you reside in an urban location where people are excited about unique art designs but do not have the time to create them themselves. By setting a fair price for your things, you may quickly make a large amount of money without much effort. In order to experience the excitement of a show-and-tell event, book a booth at a local farmer's market and arrive with some crafts that are ready to sell. The amount of individuals who arrive and a subset of those who could be interested in buying from you are both important factors in this situation.

Bring flyers to hand out to people so they can reach you through one of your social media accounts or email and check all your existing Etsy listings. Think of these events as a means of marketing for those who are not as active online but can be excited with customized products to meet their next big life event like a baby shower, birthday party, or wedding.

One downside to participating in local events is the generation of mass inventory and booth displays, topped with expenses to load and transport the inventory. You may or may not be able to sell all of the inventory depending on the size of the event, but as I said earlier, you can still make the most of this by marketing your products and building up a local clientele.

Online: Social Media

All of us are really well aware that social media has evolved into a powerful marketing tool for quite large organizations as well as small enterprises and aspiring entrepreneurs. To advertise your items, join Facebook community pages and groups for handicraft vendors and consumers to get exposure. To lure prospective consumers, insert hashtags such as for sale, product, selling, free delivery, the sample included, and other variations. When you publish items on these networks and your own Facebook page, use snappy words like "customization available at no additional cost" or "free returns if you are not happy" to capture people's attention. Make use of Twitter to offer comments from your delighted consumers in order to expand your clientele. It is possible to do this by producing a customer satisfaction survey that you can send to your purchasers through email, or by attaching a link to your Etsy listing in which you solicit online reviews and ratings from your consumers.

Another suggestion is to publish images of everything and everything you have made using "Cricut" machines, even if you do not really intend to sell what you have made. You never know who else could be interested in something that you judged unsellable in the first place.

Because you will be producing them just after the order has been made, you will be able to swiftly obtain the necessary resources after the fact and begin to work on your project immediately.

Etsy

Yes! Don't forget to check out the angel policy. You can sell items utilizing non-licensed images in the Cricut library, or you could design your graphics using illustrator or photoshop. You can't sell accredited pictures—Disney, Marvel Comics, etc. These pictures are trendy, and you'll see Etsy stores selling these kinds of images, but these stores can be closed down or perhaps sued for selling accredited prints.

Would You Market Cricut Layouts?

Yes! The Cricut angel policy permits you to sell around 10,000 layouts annually with discounts created with Provo craft solutions. There's room to increase your company and sell arrangements made using Cricut products. Just be sure that you read over the complete angel policy to ensure you are working inside.

What are the Most Lucrative Cricut Companies?

The most rewarding Cricut companies are people who provide unique products that people wish to purchase. Why waste your time creating products that nobody is considering? Instead, spend your time exploring your competitors. Learn what other crafting organizations are doing well and where they're making errors. This could enable you to locate a complete in your marketplace so you can create things with lesser competition.

Selling Finished Pieces

Next time you embark on another one of your creative journeys leading to unique creations, make two of everything, and you can quickly put the other product to sell on your Etsy shop. You would be using your "Cricut" machines for various personal projects like home décor, holiday décor, personalized clothing, and more. Additionally, you will be able to keep all of your projects on the design space application for future use, which means that if one of your designs becomes popular, you will be able to simply purchase the necessary materials and convert them into money-making products. This way, not only does your original idea for personal usage pay off, but you can make much more money than you invested in it to begin with.

Again, please spend some time researching what designs and decorations are trending in the market and use them to spark inspiration for your next project. Some of the current market trends include customized cake and cupcake toppers and watercolor designs framed as fancy wall decorations. The cake toppers can be made with cardstock, which is another beginner-friendly material, light in weight, and can be economically shipped tucked inside an envelope.

Chapter 5. Personalized Clothing and Accessories

T-shirts with cool designs and phrases are all the rage right now. Just follow a similar approach to selling vinyl and take it up a notch. You can create sample clothing with an iron-on design and market it with "can be customized further at no extra charge" or "transfer the design on your own clothing" to get traction in the market. You can buy sling bags and customize them with unique designs to be sold as finished products at a higher price than a plain boring sling bag.

Consider creating a line of products with a centralized theme like the DC Marvel characters or the "Harry Potter" movies and design custom t-shirts, hats, and even bodysuits for babies. You can create customized party favor boxes and gift bags at the request of the customer. Once your product has a dedicated customer base, you can get project ideas from them directly and quote them a price for your work.

Other Personalized Projects for Cricut

Ordinarily, it is always advisable to follow what you are good at and have passion for, which is something that will not bore you out. However, you haven't really tried out everything there is in the craft world and might not know what you could be good at or could like. Here are some ideas of projects that can be done to make money on Cricut using your Cricut Maker 3.

Wedding Décor: This is such a great area to get into as people are always getting married, therefore you could create custom signs, little tags of where people are going to sit and even personalize all the way down to the plates, napkins, cups, making flowers with felt or fabric etc.

Stickers and Decals: Stickers are great and can be used for several things, you could create stickers for businesses, custom compliment stickers for packages and a lot more. Decals can be created for cars, laptops, cell phone covers etc.

Drinkware and Tumblers: Coffee cups have always been amazing to personalize with fantastic stickers or awesome quotes. Everybody has coffee cups in their homes, so it is something people are going to be purchasing for years to come. Wine glasses are another drinkware that can be personalized just as the coffee cup. For example if you want to customize such a gift for a customer that wants to send it to a person that has moved to college, you could simply add the college logo on it or even a well-wish message. When it comes to tumblers, you could personalize them with names or wrap them up with a beautiful print like a leopard print, lovely design, or a great pattern. There are a ton of different interesting ideas when it comes to drinkwares.

T-shirts and Clothing: It is possible you could create your own different brand and have super quotes on them, layer projects, you could do adult t-shirts as well as baby wears with unique captivating designs. One great idea about t-shirts is to do the matching parent and child t-shirt as well as pajamas. You could also do t-shirts for companies adding their logo on it or for a family going for a special vacation. Still on clothing, you could make a catchy printed design for underwear or socks, print on sport jerseys for teams etc. Apparently, there is a lot to cover in the apparel department of Cricut as a business or career.

Felts Flowers and Succulents: This is something that has always been trending, and it is perfect for wedding décor, home décor or just even adding it to your project.

Nursery Décor: There are certainly lots of baby items that can be personalized and decorated, such as blankets, pants, etc. it is even possible to decorate the walls in the baby's room with flowers or have some decals to serve as wallpaper.

Wooden Signs: This is also a vast area to cover, such as personalized welcome signs as well as tags around the home for house warming gear, Christmas, Halloween etc.

Cards: Cards are a common craft that can be made special and unique with unusual designs and concepts. Cards get purchased all the time and it is really nice to have a homemade card. It varies in a wide range, such as greeting cards, Christmas cards, etc.

Acrylic Keychains and Phone Cases: This is an area that gets patronized very frequently, as everybody has keys and a cellphone. Acrylic keychains have been trendy for quite some time and there are a lot of different ways this could be done from personalizing to having a cool and unique pattern.

Chapter 6. Marketing on Social

Media

What you can do with the Cricut is almost limitless in its possibilities. Likewise, there are countless things you can make which are marketable. Independent entrepreneurship is easier than it's ever been thanks to the internet and web platforms that make selling your products a breeze.

If you're reading this, you've probably already heard of some of the platforms that make it simple to start your own business. Etsy is probably the most well-known of these platforms, and setting up a shop with them is so simple, it's almost impossible not to be interested in starting one for yourself!

With the Cricut, making countless items of every type and theme, for all occasions, is the name of the game. Doing these projects can be a huge source of joy for the avid crafter, but if you're spending the money on the materials for your projects, it might make sense for you to start generating a return on those, depending on how much you're doing and spending.

We'll cover some of the basics of what it means to go into business for yourself when you're the sole manufacturer of the goods in your store. Without having to provide a brick-and-mortar space for your shop, overhead can be so much lower than starting a shop or store is viable for people who might not have a lump sum of startup capital ready to hand.

How Do You Know the Time to Start a Shop?

If crafting is your passion, and you prefer to spend your time making items with your Cricut than you would going out or any other activity in your downtime, it could be time. If you're finding that your crafting room is getting full of projects you've made but haven't gotten to use for that special occasion yet, you might find that you could sell those items to others, make back what you spent on the materials, as well as get paid for the time and the effort it took you to put the project together in the first place!

Should I Quit My Day Job and Go All In?

The thing about selling the products you create is that, since there's no brick-and-mortar location to manage, no store hours to keep to, you can manage your sales and your projects in the spare time that you have. It is best to start your store while you have a stable source of income. This way, as your store grows, you can scale back where it's necessary to do so in your usual work schedule, to allow for more time to spend on your shop.

How Can One Make Sure People will Buy the Products?

There is a wealth of ways to market a business in today's digital age. Between social media presence, search engine optimization, and more, you can put your name everywhere it needs to be to generate interest. However, you might find that when you're starting out, it will be easiest to pick items that are not custom. Make a couple of each type of item, take stunning product photos, upload them to your store, then sell those as off-the-rack items.

As you start to generate more business, you may find that taking on the occasional custom order or commissioned item will benefit you. By and large, you will find that custom orders will take you more time and cost more to produce for less of a return. Be watchful of this, and if you find that making 100 of a general design and selling all of those is the best use of your time and resources, stick with that! There's nothing inherently wrong with taking that way, either.

Do I Need to Make Enough of Each Item in my Shop to Keep and Inventory?

The short answer to this is no. You don't have to make any more of any items that are being ordered at any given time. With the way Etsy works for sellers, you can determine how much time you have before shipping out an order, so you can make the items as they're ordered, so you can be certain you're never wasting product or letting it sit in your craft room for too long.

The only time it would be best to make any sort of inventory would be if you intend to rent a space, or booth at a tradeshow or convention. Having a presence at craft fairs, conventions, tradeshows, etc., can generate impulse buys from passing patrons that could be great for your business.

If at all possible, it's best to wait to go to such an event until you're able to narrow down your best sellers. Once you have a smattering of items you can make that are your hottest items, you can make several of each of those, and keep them at your booth or table, ready for immediate purchase!

Do I Need to Create a Shop in Order to Make Money with Cricut?

To be candid, no, you don't need to create a shop if you don't want to. Different approaches to problems may always be found, and generating money with your Cricut is just as adaptable as the items created with your Cricut machine itself. If there is someone else who runs a craft shop, you might ask them to list your items for you in exchange for a share of the profits.

You could create a partnership with a local school, community center, farmer's market, or other establishments to sell your items for you to their patrons. There are so many ways to go about getting your unique crafts into the hands of the public, and to make money off the beautiful projects you make with your Cricut system.

Making an online store for your Cricut items might be the most direct, hands-on way to generate a stream of income from the items that you make. This does not mean, however, that it's the only way, or that it's the best way for you to go about it. Test the waters, see what's available, and pick a path that is most workable for you and the business you're working to create.

How Should I Price My Items?

This, like everything else, is entirely up to you. One method of pricing is to decide on a rate you would like to be paid per hour spent on a project, multiply that rate by how many hours you spent on that project, and add it together with the costs of all the materials you used to make your project.

For instance, I would never take a full-time job that paid me fewer than $15 per hour. We'll use this as our artisan rate to start. When you grow better at what you do, as you build a larger following and as you complete each of the projects you sell, you can always alter your rates accordingly. So, with this $15 hourly rate, we'll put together a little project. Let's say I'm taking a sheet of printable vinyl, and printing an image that I own onto it. From there, I'm layering that vinyl onto a cardboard backing. Once that's done, I'm going to run it through my Cricut and make a jigsaw puzzle out of it.

Once I've made my jigsaw puzzle, I'm going to use more cardboard to make a box, which I will then decoupage. The box will be filled with the puzzle pieces, wrapped with a satin ribbon, and sold in my online store. Let's run the tally!

Cricut Printable Vinyl - $9

Cardboard Sheets - $6

Decoupage Glue - $2

Satin Ribbon - $1

1 Hour of Labor - $15.00

Artisan jigsaw puzzle - $33.00

Do not sell yourself short on your labor costs, and do not charge less than you spend on your materials, ever! That's no way to run a business, and it's no way to live. Value your time properly and charge every penny that you're worth. With how beautiful your products are, you will find people will pay your rates, and you will get rave reviews every time!

Conclusion

As you can see and learn from the examples above, Cricut machines may be used for a wide variety of projects. These instruments are well-known for their ability to operate with both thin and thick materials. Photographs may also be printed on the printer by using the Cricut modeling tools that are included with the machine. As a result, clip art, printed photos, and other images may be cut out using a Cricut machine.

It is possible to utilize a Cricut gadget for a range of jobs. When it comes to die-cutting, their ease of use and practicality have made them popular options among consumers. A Cricut machine is thus necessary for those who work in the crafting industry on a regular basis. The most appropriate cutting machine for a novice would be one that has a large number of features and is straightforward to use.

Each of these Cricut cutting machines are fantastic, and they both offer unique functionality that ensures great quality and efficiency in the cutting process. They also have innovative and cutting-edge features that are designed to stimulate your creativity. Choose the Cricut machine that has the features you want. Each of the Cricut machines listed above has its own set of features, so choose which one best meets your requirements.

Book 4:

CRICUT PROJECT IDEAS

VOL. I

Table of Contents

Chapter 1: Some examples of Cricut project ideas

Let's do some Cricut projects. But, before we get into the specifics of the designs, there are a few simple steps to nearly all Cricut projects.

- You'll begin by creating a design for your idea in the Design Space.

- Place your cutting mat on top of your material.

- Feed the material and tangle through the device.

- Press the cut button.

- Keep an eye on the device while it does many of the complicated tasks.

- Take the tangle out of the machine.

- Carefully remove the design.

- Remove any unwanted waste of material.

- Assemble if necessary.

1.1. Penguin Christmas card

Materials

- Reindeer Penguin

- Cardstock in occasion tints

- Silver and Red Cricut Pens

- Glue

- 12" x 12" Standard Grip Cricut tangle

- Cricut Explore Air 2 Cutting machine.

Instructions

- The cut patterns cling to the on-screen guidelines.

- Glue all of the penguin examples together and use craft print for topping on it, then slice out the penguin design to provide a dimensional extension to your card.

- Paste the square example at the front of the card and try to cover the square example window as far as possible.

- Cut out another inside square if desired.

- Gather the envelopes.

- Use a smaller heart as a sticker to close the envelope by pasting it to the convergence of the snowflake pattern.

1.2. Cricut Iron-On project (T-shirt making)

Materials

- Iron-On

- T-Shirt of your choice

- Parchment Paper

- Small Towel

- Weeder and Scraper

- Cricut EasyPress/Regular Iron

- Cricut Explore Air 2.

Instructions

- Upload the design to Cricut space.

- Weld and resize it by following the cutting instructions.

- Load Mat with Iron-On material

- Load Fine point Blade.

- Remove the pattern from the mat and weed it out.

- Transfer to a T-shirt and peel off whilst the back is still warm.

- Let it sit for 24 hours before cleaning it. Bleach should never be included.

1.3. DIY Canvas art

Materials

- Canvas

- Paint Brush

- Screwdriver

- Pliers

- Craft Knife

- Rag

- Free Downloadable Cut File

- Iron-on in Black

- Iron or Cricut EasyPress

- Staple Gun

- Wood Stain

- Weeding tools (optional)

- Cricut Machine

Instructions

- To detach the canvas from the frame, turn the canvas on to the rear and eliminate any staples keeping it in position using a screwdriver and pliers.

- Remove the cord and turn the frame around to the front. Enable to rest for a few seconds if there is some stain paint, then clean away any excess with a rag and put aside to dry entirely.

- Open Cricut Design and upload the free downloadable Cut file.

- Put the iron-on shiny side on the mat and mirror the image. The picture could then be cut.

- Clean out the extra iron-on from the edges of the words and the centers of any characters. Weeding tools make it simpler, but they're not essential.

- Position the weeded pattern on the canvas's front. Fix it with an iron or the Cricut EasyPress.

- Tear away the protective layer to expose the perfectly adhered design on the canvas.

- Fix the canvas in the frame by putting it in the middle of the stained frame and then flipping it over. Staple it to the rear of the frame in some places using a staple device.

- Cut out all of the extra canvas with a craft knife.

1.4. Infusible Ink Tote Bag

Materials

- Green StandardGrip Cricut Mat

- EasyPress 2 (or heat press)

- EasyPress 2 Mat

- Heat-resistant tape

- Tweezers

- Lint roller

- White cardstock

- Butcher paper

- Cricut Infusible Ink Blank Tote Bag

- Cricut Infusible Ink Transfer Sheet

- Cricut Explore Air 2

Instructions

- In design space, create the design. If you are designing for the first time, go for something easy like this amusing "World's Okayest Adult" badge pic.

Figure 3.5: World's Okayest Adult logo

- Reduce the scale to suit your tote. If you're using the medium EasyPress 2, it's best to render it 8.5″ x 8.5″ because you have more wiggle space along the side. In the top right corner, click Make It. Don't forget to mirror your picture when you're at the Prepare screen.

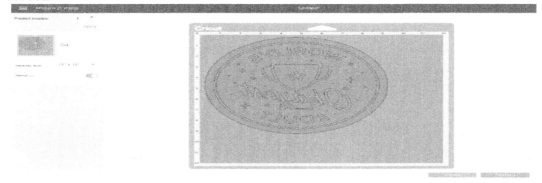

Figure 3.6: Layout Setting

- In the Make screen, use Infusible Ink Transfer Sheet should be used as your material. Be sure you're using the Fine Point Blade.

Figure 3.7: Material Setting

- Place the liner side of the sheet on the cutting pad. The sheet is extremely light grey, as you'll see! It's almost off-white in color. However, as you will note, the ink does brighten up when heated.

- Then, using Wild Rose Explore Air 2, feed it into your device and cut it out.

- Weed the infusible ink. The Infusible Ink has a paper ink sheet and a thin paper liner, similar to the dual-layer of paper.

Figure 3.8: Design placement on cutting pad

- Until you begin your transfer, prepare your tote bag. Begin by placing your EasyPress Mat within a tote bag and covering it all with a white piece of cardstock. If your EasyPress mat bleeds, the cardstock will help to keep it clean.

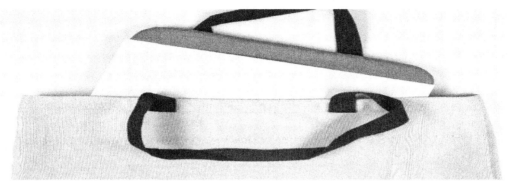

Figure 3.9: Covering the Mat within Tote bag

- Clear all the dust and dirt from the bag using a lint roller. This would ensure that the transfer is as clean as possible.

Figure 3.10: Setting up the bag.

- Move Cricut Infusible Ink with The EasyPress. Second, use butcher paper to cover your blank tote bag. To further flatten the surface and dry all moisture within the bag, pre-heat your bag before applying your switch. Allow cooling fully after pressing for 15 seconds.

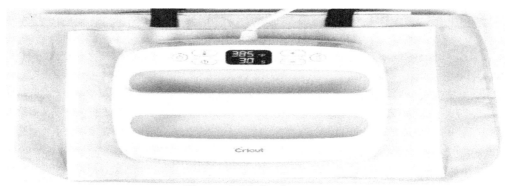

Figure 3.11: Preheating

- Add your transfer after your bag has fully cooled. If you're worried about the transfer shifting, seal it with a piece of heat-resistant tape.

Figure 3.12: Embossing the design

- Cover the top of the transfer with butcher paper again. Then, using light but constant pressure, carefully click your EasyPress onto your design for 40 seconds. Please ensure the EasyPress is fully covering the transfer.

Figure 3.13: Infusible Ink Tote Bag

- Allow the transfer to cool until cautiously picking it up—it may not stick to your bag.

Chapter 2: Writing and Drawing with Cricut

Many of your Cricut projects, including pen and ink drawings and coloring page designs, will include hand-painted accents. Enable your Cricut machine to do the job for you if you like the style of hand-drawn art but don't want to create it yourself.

There are several unique pen colors to pick from, and a brand-new range of black pens is now available. The Cricut Pens make it simple to give your writing a more hand-drawn look.

2.1. What resources are required for drawing and writing?

Cricut machine – either of the Cricut Explore, Cricut Maker, or Cricut Joy machines should suffice.

Cricut Design Space – Using a Cricut Access account makes it easier to use the fonts and functionality. You will still use photographs and fonts from your archive instead of paying for them.

Cricut Pens - The basic fine black ink pen is included with any Cricut machine. With only this single pen, you can produce a plethora of fantastic designs. Different types of Cricut pens are listed below:

- o **Fine tip pens** are available in a variety of colors. These are ideal for applying accents to your artwork. The tips are tiny enough to illustrate minor details while maintaining a clean line. In general, 0.3 and 0.4 sizes are ideal for about anything.

- o **Calligraphy pens** are available in a range of styles, including up to two calligraphy pen nib size range. This will encourage you to use your Cricut pen art to make a fancy calligraphy look.

- o **Glitter pens** resembles ballpoint pens and with a smooth paint glide to the paint, resulting in a colorful glitter effect with a clear pattern.

- o **Metallic pens** normally have a much larger tip and draw in a similar manner to a medium size marker.

2.2. The Cricut Writing tool Palette

Simply mark the line as "draw" in the Design space to produce a painting or writing line. To do so, follow these steps:

- Choose the picture layer from which you like to illustrate. If it's a pen, scissors, or scanner, click the layer icon. The palette would appear, allowing you to choose "draw". After that, you can also select a color for that project layer.

- You have the option of selecting the color where you'd like your design to appear on display. If all the pictures needed to be sketched using the identical black pen, for example, choose the same paint as well as pen for each style in your final piece.

- You'll be prompted to adjust your pen colors as required when you configure Cricut to build your model inside Design Space. Any color you choose can result in a notification telling you when to change your tool color when Cricut is working on it.

2.3. Drawing Projects

2.3.1 What are the steps to creating your own butterfly coloring page?

Materials

- White Cardstock

- Butterfly SVG design by Jen Goode

- Colored pencils (optional)

- Cricut Pen

- Cricut machine (Explore, Air or Maker)

Instructions

- Open Cricut Design Space and upload the butterfly design.

- All of the layers should be set to drawing/writing. To make complete designs, group the like pieces together. Each wing has its own design layer; you can join all four parts together to make a group or "weld" them together to make a single item.

- To make the picture you like, move the designs around.

- You may make several butterflies by duplicating bits. To build different looks, add extra parts to certain butterflies and layer separate draw lines.

- If you've found a style you want, pick the whole canvas (everything) and join all of the elements into a single package. Once you move to the "create it" mat, this will keep the whole design in position.

- Create it by pressing the "make it" button and following the on-screen directions.

2.3.2 How to print, cut and draw with your Cricut.

Materials

- Paper

- Cricut pens

- Printer synced with your Cricut.

- Cricut cutting machine – any version will work.

- Cricut Design Space

Instructions

- Select the appropriate design.

- Attach the printed painting and the drawing together.

- Use a range of drawing patterns to complement the printed designs. Here are few suggestions:

- Add a shiny drawing touch to written picture borders or outlines. In Cricut Design Room, duplicate the outline of a printed picture and transform it into a drawing or writing. Until sending the project to the mat, apply the line to the written form.

- Convert a few of the cut elements into drawing lines to give the designs a special look. Since you can't flatten a drawing line, make sure you flatten any of the written bits before attaching the drawing line.

- To add a finishing touch, add additional drawing accents like boundaries or lines to the final printed parts.

- Create art drawing patterns with Cricut.

2.3.3 Use the Cricut to build layered designs

When you want to make hand-drawn artwork with your Cricut, but the designs don't go together well, making paper layers will help. Certain art designs make for several layers, whilst others do not, so pay attention to the designs you choose to create with layers.

- **What are the requirements for creating layered designs?**

  o Layered draw designs have to have a cut and a draw/write line. You'll need to search for art that either allows you to cut around the painting or can be edited to allow you to cut across the drawing line.

- **Creating cut layers**

  o Many of the art files have different layers for the design, such that cutting and painting can be done. This isn't the case for all art. To make layered draw art, you will need to build your own cut layers sometimes.

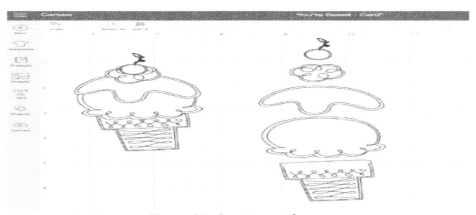

Figure 4.1: Creating cut layers.

  o If the art you choose to use doesn't have these separate layers, you'll have to make them yourself or choose another piece of art. Here's an explanation (*figure 4.2*) of what you might be looking for. Each section of the ice cream cone has its own layer. As desired, you can alter each layer separately.

- **Editing draw layers**

- You may choose to create a design but not have all of the specifications, or you may want to adjust the colors used in various aspects of the design. For this, use contour. The Contour function may be used to edit several drawing styles. Simply pick the layer you would like to update, press Contour, and then cover the parts of the drawing you don't want to create.

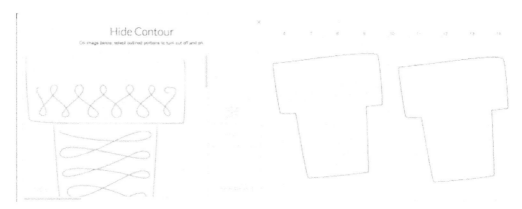

Figure 4.2: Editing with Contour function

- **Attaching drawn art to each layer**

    - Draw and write lines must always be connected to a cut shape; otherwise, they will simply draw on the page and will not be cut off. You don't need to attach anything if you have a card and just wish to write on it. For all other times, make sure the draw lines are still connected to the shape you expect them to be drawn on.

Figure 4.3: colored and uncolored artwork

o In certain instances, you will flatten all of the layers and then sketch on the flattened artwork as well. Experiment with the different solutions to see which one fits well with the project you're working on. Use various shades of paper to add painting effects, or only use plain white paper to draw the star. Here's an example (Figure 4.4) of the same artwork in both colored and uncolored versions.

Chapter 3: Cricut Project Ideas

There are about as many Cricut ideas as there are humans, multiplied by the materials available. You can make great DIY crafts for every purpose with a Cricut Maker, Cricut Explore, or the adorable Cricut Joy.

Let's have a look at several projects that range from simple to difficult.

3.1. Tassels

Tassels may be used in a variety of ways. These are extremely simple to produce and can be made to fit any task. Use them as a keyring or zipper pick, add them to the sides of pillows or covers, hang them from a rope to create a banner, and a thousand other items! You may even make them out of leather or faux leather for a more elegant look. Tassels look great on almost everything.

Materials

- Fabric mat

- 12" x 18" fabric rectangles

- Glue gun

- Cricut machine

Instructions

- Launch Design Space to begin a new design.

- Click the "Image" icon in the bottom left-hand corner and type "tassel" into the search box.

- Press "Insert" after selecting the illustration of a rectangle with lines on either side.

- Arrange fabric on the mat and use the Cricut to cut out the pattern.

- Take the fabric off the mat and save the excess square.

- Beginning from the uncut side, position the material face down and roll tightly. As required, untangle the fringe.

- To attach the tassel at the top, use some waste fabric and a hot glue stick.

- Use your beautiful tassels to decorate anything you like!

3.2. Paw Print Socks

Socks are the epitome of comfort. Small paw prints add a cool, secret decoration to the base of your socks. Every time you cuddle up, show off your affection towards pets. You can do this with about every small style or even add text to the base of your foot to add a quotation. You can select any kind of socks you choose. Please ensure the sock and vinyl colors contrast for easy reading. Or, for a hidden design, make them all in the same color! Under certain lighting, the vinyl shine will contrast with the fabric. You'll require your Cricut EasyPress or iron for this since it uses heat transfer vinyl.

Materials

- Socks

- Weeding tool or pick

- Scrap cardboard

- Heat transfer vinyl

- Cutting mat

- Cricut EasyPress or iron

- Cricut machine

Instructions

- Build a new project in Cricut Design Space.

- Check for "paw prints" using the "Photo" button in the bottom left-hand corner.

- Select your preferred paw prints and click "Insert."

- Send the pattern to the Cricut by placing the iron-on material on the mat.

- To eliminate excess material, use a pick or weeding tool.

- Take the material from the mat and stuff the socks with scrap cardboard.

- Put the iron-on material onto the socks' bottoms.

- To attach it to the iron-on material, use EasyPress.

- Take the cardboard from the socks after they have cooled.

- Put on your adorable paw print socks!

3.3. Monogrammed Drawstring Bag

Drawstring bags are simple to use and carry. They're just as easy to produce as they are to use!   These bags can be kept on hand for anyone in your family to pick and go as required. You may use monograms to distinguish them, or you can use a different pattern on each one to modify it for a certain purpose or simply to decorate it. This can also be used as gift bags! The designs are made of heat transfer vinyl, so you'll need your Cricut EasyPress or iron for this project.

Materials

- Heat transfer vinyl

- Two matching rectangles of fabric

- Weeding tool or pick

- Cutting mat

- Needle and thread

- Ribbon

- Cricut machine

- Cricut EasyPress or iron

Instructions

- Build a new project in Cricut Design Space.

- Check for "monogram" using the "Image" icon in the bottom left-hand corner.

- Select the monogram you want to use and press "Insert."

- Place the shiny liner side of the iron-on material on the mat and give the pattern to the Cricut.

- To eliminate excess material, use the weeding tool or a pick.

- Remove the monogram out of the mat.

- The monogram should be centered on your material and moved down a couple of inches, so it doesn't get rolled up as the ribbon is created.

- The pattern should be ironed onto the fabric.

- Put the two rectangles along such that the fabric's outside side is faced inward.

- Leave a seam allowance when you sew along with the corners. Let the top open and stop it a few inches below the top.

- Fold the bag's top back until the stitches are reached.

- Sew around the folded edge's bottom, keeping the sides open.

- Turn bag's right side out.

- The ribbon should be threaded through the loop at the top of the bag.

- Bring what you need in your fresh drawstring pocket!

3.4. Customized Pillow

A simple concept that is often requested and quick to personalize. Make the pillow of your dreams!

Materials

- Insert Cricut Access

- Protective Sheet Pillow Cover

- Glitter Iron-On Vinyl

- Iron-On

- Cricut Easypress Mat

- Cricut Machine

Instructions

- From the Home tab of the Cricut Design Space, select "New Project."

- Click the text icon in the lower right corner of the page and choose the font you like. Fill in your name and adjust the size of the box corner to fit your pillow.

- To add an additional bit of text for your Est. Year, choose the Text button. Drag and arrange your last name properly.

- Choose all textboxes at the same time and hit the attach button. It will link the two text boxes, allowing for precise cutting.

- The screen appears as you click the "Make It" icon. Allow that the Mirror is turned on.

- To switch on and off the mirror setting, click the image in the upper left corner. The image above appears on the computer. Turn the "off" switch on.

- Press the Mirror button; the mat will now reflect your mirrored image, and you're ready to load your Iron-On Vinyl shiny side down onto your mat. Follow the instructions by clicking and dragging.

- Weed the excess vinyl and center the pillow cover design once the design has been sliced.

- Use the Easypress Settings Chart to set the timer and temperature for your material.

- Use the Iron-On Protection Sheet to cover the structure, then top it with the Easypress and press the Cricut button. When it has beeped, remove it. Heat for 10 to 15 seconds on the other side of your pillow cover.

- Enable the iron-on to cool before removing the sheet.

3.5. Cricut Gift Boxes

What is the point of creating crafts if you don't gift them? You may even create your own box designs after you've become more comfortable with the Design Space software – nothing beats training for honing a talent. Let's have a look at how you should get started designing your own gift boxes right now.

Materials

- Scoring wheel

- Cardstock (Glitter or of your choice)

- Glue

- Cricut machine

Instructions

- Launch Cricut Design Space and choose "New Project," then import the SVG file patterns you've searched or downloaded. Alternately, start creating your own box patterns.

- Start with the pillowcase package, which is probably the easiest to create for a novice. Using the upper formatting panel in Design Space, resize the patterns to suit the box's expected size. If you're producing more than one box, make sure to click "Ungroup" to distinguish the prototypes that need to be cut and assembled separately. Before submitting the design to cutting, make sure to adjust the Line form to "Score" for any sections of the model that should be folded. After you've finished scoring the lines which have to be folded, pick the whole pattern and click on "Attach," then finish sizing, if necessary, before clicking "Make it."

- When deciding on cutting settings under "Make it," use cardstock as your chosen material. You should start cutting after you've arranged the material and the cutting pad.

- Assemble the box(es) you'll be using. You won't need to use adhesive to hold the pieces of the box intact if you use light materials like paper or standard cardstock. If you're using glitter cardstock or similar materials, though, you'll need to glue all of the pieces of the package together except the portion that's meant to seal it.

- Begin putting together your package, gluing the pieces that need to be sealed while you move. To help it go smoother and more efficiently, use tacky glue or a glue gun. And your box is all set!

3.6. Personalized Christmas Ornaments

Materials

- Heat-Resistant Tape

- Cardstock (white)

- Sublimation Ornaments in Blank Form

- Butcher paper

- Mat and EasyPress 2

- Explore Air 2 Machine or Cricut Maker

- Buffalo Check Cricut Infusible Ink Transfer Sheet

- Cloth without any lint

Instructions

- Create your own personalized holiday ornaments by starting a new design in Cricut Design Space.

- For the front and back of each ornament, place two 2.81″ circles. Using the slice feature to generate negative space photographs of the designs within the circle after adding your favorite holiday photos and custom text to the circle.

- Cut your designs with your Cricut machine (ensure to mirror your picture before cutting!) and weed the unwanted Infusible Ink with your fingertips or tweezers.

- Remove any dust, dirt, or smudges from the ornament's surface with a lint-free fabric.

- Apply Infusible Ink on both sections of the blank ornament and cover with heat-resistant tape.

- Preheat the EasyPress 2 to 400ºF and set the timer for 240 seconds. Cover with another layer of butcher paper after placing the ornaments on top of the butcher paper.

- Place the EasyPress 2 on top of the decorations for 240 seconds; just don't press down! Place the EasyPress 2 back on its base after the loop is over, then carefully peel the top layer of butcher paper.

3.7 Christmas Tea Towels

Christmas tea towels are a simple and quick way to get started with the Cricut cutting unit. Simply use heat transfer vinyl to provide almost limitless design options.

Materials

- Tea towel with a deer silhouette

- Tea towel "Merry and Bright."

- flour sack towels (white)

- Cut files and iron-on for Christmas tea towels.

- Tool for weeding

- press cloth or parchment paper.

- Iron or EasyPress

- Cricut Explore Air 2 or Cricut Maker

Instructions

- In Design Space, open the Christmas tea towel cut file(s).

- Adjust the sizes and colors to your liking. Don't neglect to mirror the text while cutting the iron-on vinyl for your Christmas tea towels.

- Choose the materials. The cutting material on the Cricut Maker is selected directly in Design Space; many of the most popular cutting material choices may appear.

- With the weeder unit, remove any negative space from the designs.

- Place the patterns on the towel with the liners and see where you like them.

- Set the EasyPress's temperature and timer according to the instructions for the material you're ironing on and the material you're ironing on to. Preheat the tea towel by ironing it to prevent any wrinkles. Cover the pattern with the press cloth or parchment paper and press down tightly for the period shown on the map. To begin the timer, press the right-hand Cricut button. Enable the liners to cool down for a moment after the timer goes off before trying to peel them off. Replace the filler and click for another 5–10 seconds if some aspect of the pattern starts to pull up.

Chapter 4: How to make Paper projects with Cricut?

Paper is readily available and offered in a wide variety of colors, textures, sizes, and finishes. It has many applications. The options are endless when it comes to cards, drawings, and custom designs. A few of the most common Paper Projects will be discussed in this chapter.

4.1 Paper Flowers

Flowers are lovely, but they don't last long until they wilt. However, paper ones will last you forever! It can be used as decoration for an event or gathering. Brides on a budget will also use this instead of an extravagant flower arrangement to walk down the aisle! In the Cricut Design Space, you'll find a plethora of flower models. You can also look for more on the internet or try your hand at designing your own. A bouquet may consist of a single form of a flower, the same flower in various colors, a combination of flowers, or a variation of flowers in the same color. It all relies on the feel and look you want to achieve, so go for which approach appeals to you.

Materials

- Light Grip Mat
- Card Stock Paper
- Adhesive
- Cricut Air 2 Machine

Instructions

- In Design Space, enter "Flower" in the Search Field. There are several flower options; most will perform as long as they have a stable center. It is entirely up to you to make your decision!
- Open the project while selecting the flower that you like.
- Copy and paste flower (5 times), making each flower shorter than the last when you paste it in place. This will give the final product complexity and texture by creating different sizes. Make sure your Cricut machine is set to cardstock after you've posted all of the flower designs.
- A paper should be lined up according to the layout/mat.
- Submit the Project for Cutting
- Remove and gently lift Flowers from the Mat.
- Cut flowers can be lined up in order of size, from largest to smallest, so they can be stacked.
- Petals should be bent upwards from the middle. Start with the largest paper flower and work your way through the other four, twisting each one a little further each time.
- Using your adhesive, glue the flowers together. Position the flowers on top of each other, beginning from the largest flower and working the way down to the smallest.

4.2 Coffee Cup Gift Card Holder

Materials

- LightGrip Mat
- Cardstock
- Your gift card
- Corrugated cardboard
- SVG design
- Tacky glue
- A pen
- Cricut Maker cutting machine, Cricut Explore or Cricut Joy

Instructions

- Open Cricut Design Space and import the coffee cup (gift card holder) SVG cut file.
- Place your materials on the LightGrip cutting pad, choose the appropriate cutting substance, load your blade as instructed, and cut your pattern.
- Take all of the material from the Mat.
- Attach the lid to the inner cup's top.
- You may either insert the gift card into the slits or glue it into the cardholder bag. To use the pocket, lay the card pocket face down, position your gift card on top of it, and properly glue around it, as seen in the picture below. Pick up the pocket and card and put them together on your inner cup, pressing down.
- Fold the outer cup sheet in half and glue the lower part of the outer cup, as well as one of the outer cup's edges. Fold the paper back up and hold it until the glue is dry.
- Fold the wrapping over the outside of the cup and glue all edges.
- On the sticker, write the recipient's name. Glue the top and bottom labels together, then to the wrap. Your cup is all set!

4.3 Paper Butterfly Bouquet

Materials

- Flower stem wire
- 2-by-12-inch cardstock in multiple colors
- 1 Cricut 12-by-12-inch LightGrip Adhesive Cutting Mat
- Cricut Explore Air 2

Instructions

- Upload the design you've chosen to Design Space. Click "Customize" to update the project, then use the options in the Edit bar to make improvements. Click "Make It" or "Continue."
- Using the StandardGrip pad, position the first piece of cardstock. To load the machine, follow these instructions: Select "Cardstock" on the SmartSet Dial. Clamp B should be loaded with a fine-point razor. Click the "Load / Unload" button after loading the Mat.
- Cut by pressing the blinking "Go" icon. Remove the Mat. Remove the wasted material, then raise the individual butterflies with the spatula from the simple toolset if necessary.
- Repeat the above step when Load each fresh sheet of cardstock onto the cutting pad, then feed it into the machine as directed.
- Sort the butterfly pieces into groups based on color and shape.
- To make the butterflies double-sided, hot glue the contrasting bits together.
- Attach all the butterflies to a piece of decorative stem string or floral wire.
- Arrange the flower wires in your hand before placing them in a vase. (For a more comfortable catch, use decorative foam in your vessel).

Chapter 5: Tips And Trick

Using a Cricut is a thrilling experience. For a novice, it may even be intimidating and daunting. These 28 Cricut Tricks and Secrets can save your sanity and help you remain more organized along the way, whether you're a newcomer or a professional Cricut crafter.

5.1 Cricut Tricks and Secrets

1. Peel the mat instead of material

While it can sound natural to peel the material (vinyl, cardstock, etc.) away from the surface, it is simply preferable to softly curl and peel the mat away from the stuff. This helps to save the art supplies from being

so distorted.

2. For vinyl storage, use IKEA plastic bags.

IKEA plastic bag storage holders are another favorite Cricut hacks that have gained some attention in recent years. They're great for keeping vinyl rolls. You can even get some on the internet!

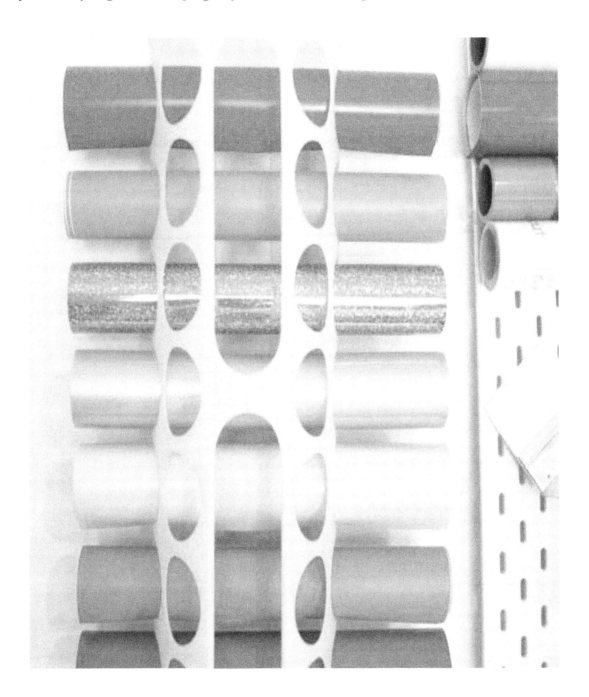

3. Tin foil should be used to sharpen the razor.

Sharpening the fine-point blade with tin foil will quickly prolong its life! In reality, using tin foil will extend the blade's life by three times! Remove the blade from the clamp and pass the edge 10-12 times through the tin foil with the blade to sharpen it.

4. keep your knives in the Cricut.

This could seem self-evident, but as a novice Cricut user, you may have no idea that the interior of your system could store the blades and small tools in a dust-free, secure manner.

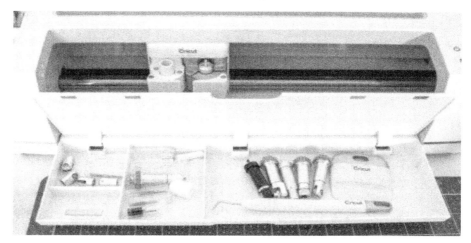

5. Pick up little fragments from your pad or pattern with a lint roller (Works for glitter too)

You should quickly catch the excess little bits on a lint roller if you have an elaborate pattern cut out on paper or vinyl to save time!

It's still great for picking up stray glitter on your desk.

6. In spite of using Cricut pens for your laptop, use pen adapters.

The ability to have your Cricut machine compose for you is a fantastic function. You'll actually wish you could use pens rather than Cricut pens at some stage.

The good news is that if you have an Explore 2 or later, you can buy pen adapters that will enable you to use almost any brand of a pen! Sharpies, brush pens, and more are all available!

How to Use ALL these Pens with Your Cricut!

1. Sharpie Fine Point
2. Sharpie Ultra Fine Point
3. Sharpie Pen Art Pen
4. Pilot Precise
5. Bic Marking
6. Bic Cristal
7. Sakura Gelly Roll
8. Amaza Gel Pens
9. Sharpie Oil-Based Paint
10. Uni-ball Signo UM-153
11. Crayola Fine Line Marker
12. Crayola Super Tip
13. Crayola Detailing Gel Pen
14. Tombow Duel Brush Pens

7. For vinyl remnants, use a nail polish tray.

One of most favorite Cricut hacks is this one! When weeding, get a cheap nail polish holder to catch tiny vinyl bits.

8. Inkscape is a free program that allows you to create your own SVG cut files.

SVG files for Design Space can be found for free or purchased by Cricut Access. So what if you had your own?

After all, there are occasions when there is a need to introduce a specific vision to life or customize an object. Inkscape is a free, open-source software for creating SVG files from nothing or converting images to layered SVG files.

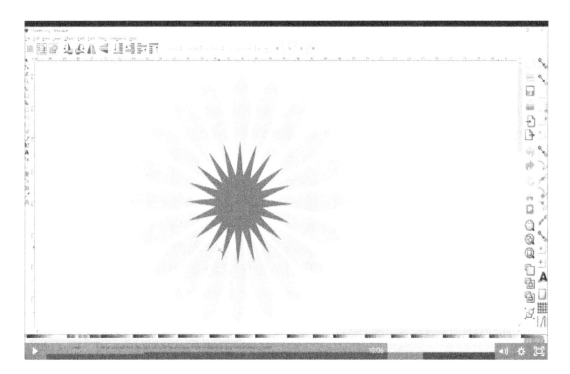

9. Converting a picture to an SVG is as simple as clicking a button

If you aren't ready to learn how to build your own SVG files, use the one-click picture to SVG converter instead.

10. Use a pegboard to keep all of your Cricut materials organized

Pegboards are vital for keeping supplies ordered, and you can save money by using unused wall space! These can be used at Amazon or on IKEA. Plus, Cricut hacks like this really help to make your craft room look nice.

11. Baby wipes may be used to clean your mat. Resticky the mat with Easy Tack

Cleaning the dirt off of recycled Cricut mats with baby wipes will give them a new lease on existence. You may even re-sticky every mat for another 5-10 uses by spraying it with a few coats of Easy Tack.

12. To hold vinyl rolls tight, use slap bracelets.

If you have a lot of vinyl, then keep the rolls in a variety of places. Slap bracelets are an inexpensive way to keep vinyl rolls intact.

13. Sort the vinyl into wood bins by type.

It's important to keep track of your vinyl styles (iron-on, textured, adhesive, etc.). Bins may be a convenient way to organize items by category and mark each bin for easy identification.

14. Trim vinyl with a smooth edge to prevent rough corners.

If you're not patient, vinyl is one of the materials that can easily be thrown away. Trimming the vinyl before cutting can help hold the edges straight and reduce waste.

15. Discover fantastic SVG freebies

Free SVG files for Design Space can be listed on Pinterest searches, among other sites. There is a huge Freebie Vault at Abbi Kirsten Collections of over 150 free SVG and printable models!

16. For tougher fabrics, use painter's tape

Painters tape will be your best buddy if your things are rolling around on your mat. It's particularly relevant when working with wood and chipboard.

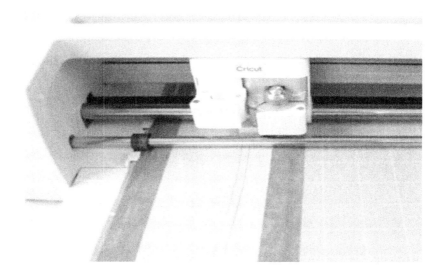

17. When adding vinyl to angled surfaces, cut slits in the transfer tape.

On a curved wall, how can you get the vinyl to be smooth?

Aside from practice, one technique is to make slits along the edges of the transfer tape. This gives the tape some wiggle room when you position the pattern.

18. Use cheat sheets to help you remember what each feature does.

Understanding Cricut terminology and the features in Design Space may be difficult to remember; a glossary cheat sheet may be very useful. You can also get it online.

19. Use a magazine holder to store vinyl remnants.

Don't throw out the odd and ends of vinyl! Small cuts can also be made for them. To see what you have to deal from, keep your scraps in a plain magazine holder.

20. Make use of a printable environment guide

Trying to recall any of those content settings or custom settings, much as Design Space features is almost difficult! There is a free guide on the subject that you can find inside the Freebie Vault!

21. On wood, use iron-on vinyl (HTV).

Well, indeed! Iron-on vinyl should be used on wood! To make it easier, Cricut has heat guidance. The look of heat transfer vinyl to that of adhesive vinyl is preferred mostly.

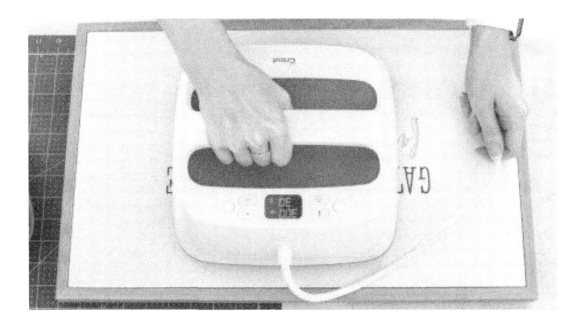

22. Use the Cricut Easy Mini-Press to apply iron-on vinyl to tumblers.

In 2019, Cricut launched the Easypress Micro, a miniature variant of the Easypress. This little gadget is so adorable and useful that it also allows you to iron on vinyl to your tumblers!

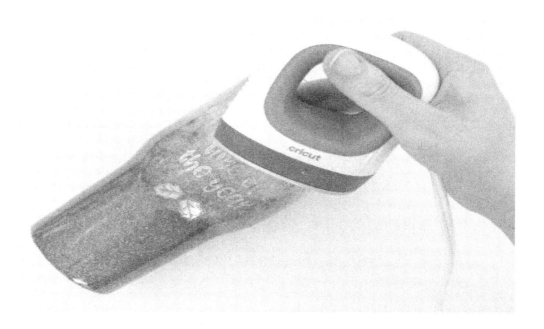

23. Freebies can be found in the Cricut Design Room.

Did you realize that every week, Cricut releases a new package of freebies that anybody can use, even if they don't have Cricut Access?! Freebies can be found under Images > Filter > Freebies!

24. Understand where to look for the right fabrics

It can take a long time and a lot of trial and error to figure out where to find the best-priced Cricut products. You can take help from the internet regarding this.

25. Use the internet to find free fonts.

You're losing out if you haven't yet mastered the strength of downloading free fonts for your Cricut. Check out the internet for the top 60 free and paid fonts, as well as exclusive Christmas font posts!

26. Import specialty projects to build a room using character maps

It's one thing to download fonts, but it's quite another to learn how to make a word appear like a million bucks! It took me a while to figure out that you can navigate those unique scrolly letters using your computer's "character charts" or "glyphs."

1. Go to your PC's "search" function and look for "character map" or "character viewer" on the Mac.
2. Pick your preferred font from the drop-down menu.
3. Scroll down before you reach the letter you're looking for.
4. Pick it with a click, then copy it.
5. In Design Space, paste the font character into the text box.

27. Maintain a list of your favorite vinyl records.

There is so much vinyl that it's difficult to keep track of them all! There are several styles, textures, and labels of vinyl to keep track of. To keep track, keep pieces of vinyl on a metal ring labeled with the brand and form of vinyl so you can still locate your favorite vinyl!

28. Keep supplies and machines in storage carts.

It's important to keep the supplies and machinery secure. A storage rolling cart is one of the favorite ways to do this! Check out your nearest Michaels shop!

5.2 Mat Maintenance and Longevity

Since the mats are costly, you will want to retain them in service for a long time. The best way to extend the existence of a mat is to treat it carefully and properly. Here are some tips about how to take control of these mats:

- After each use, replace the transparent cover/film on the sheet. Which will keep the mat clean and free of dirt and dust.
- Use a lint roller to remove any substance debris from the mat surface during each use.
- Use non-alcoholic wipes to clean the mat.
- Wash the mats with soapy water, except for the silk mat. The cotton mat is unlike any other mat in that it cannot be washed with water.
- Using a scraper, clean any object debris from the mat surface except the cloth mat.

5.3 Cricut Maker Specialty Equipment

Aside from the blades, there are other specialized instruments for purposes other than cutting.

Markers and pens

There is a space for markers and pens next to the blade housing. If you want to design greeting cards and want to use elegant fonts, this is the place to go. The Cricut is compatible with a wide range of pens and markers. Markers and pens must be purchased separately.

Scoring Wheel

This is a one-of-a-kind feature. This scoring wheel is your buddy if you don't need to cut a pattern but only need to fold a piece of material. This feature can be used for a variety of things, like creating personalized crates and making a Greeting card.

Single and double scoring tips are the two forms of scoring tips available. Depending on the project, you will use the same housing with all styles of tips.

Fast Swap Housing and Helpful Tips

This is sole housing that can be used for a variety of feature tips. The tips that can be used colloquially with this housing are explained in the following section.

Foil Transfer Tip

This is one of the most recent Cricut Maker functions. This is used to embellish and bling up the finished products. It's designed to be used with foil covers.

Deboss tip

This tip is similar to the engraving tip, but it is designed for finer, lighter materials. Foil, dense card paper, and basswood may all be decorated with it.

Engrave tip

This tip may be used to engrave texts or monograms on a variety of items. Plastic mats, leather and metal sheets are the best materials for this. With this tip, you will make the projects more special.

Perforation Tip

Tear-off materials are often used for a project. The perforation tip is used for this reason. This tip works well for lightweight fabrics.

Wavy tip

This tip can come in handy when creating greeting cards. This results in wavy edges, which provide a decorative touch. It may be used to embellish card corners, as well as iron-on vinyl and other textured sheets.

BOOK 5:

CRICUT PROJECT IDEAS

VOL. II

Table of Contents

Chapter 1: Cricut Projects Ideas II

If you own a Cricut, you are well aware of the wide range of options available. Cricut Print Then Cut is one of the best features. It makes using a Cricut much more flexible by allowing you to cut custom images created outside of Design Space.

1.1 DIY Wood Burned Ornaments Cricut Craft

What You'll Need

- Wood Slices

- Heat Gun

- Scorch Marker

- Heat Protector Mat

- Transfer Tape

- Removable Vinyl or Stencil

- Brush and Mod Podge

- Cutting machine (use a Cricut)

- Hot Glue Gun and Ribbon

- SVG Cut Files

The Scorch Marker is truly incredible. You put the marker where you intend to make the wood-burning and by using a heat gun to change the color to a wood-burnt look. You can use a heat gun to try to warm it up. But don't use a hairdryer or heat press as both of these have failed miserably.

1.2 Wood Burned Ornament: A Step-by-Step Guide

Step 1: Making a stencil

You might skip this move if you're decent at freehand. To make ornaments look nice, used the Cricut for cutting stencil vinyl.

You are free to design ornaments of your own or whatever you like with SVG cut images.

Except for these, which are on the top of the list of SVG during twelve Days of Christmas, all are described in alphabetical order. "Jesus is the Reason," The nativity scene, and Merry Christmas are the themes mostly used.

The designs will be larger and illuminated when you import them into the design applications, such as Cricut Design Room. For guidance on how to upload files and photographs to design a room, read chapter five of this book.

The first step is to adjust the color of all the prototypes to a single color. About the fact that the stencil vinyl used is blue, you can also go for black. It doesn't matter what color they are, but they all should be of the same color.

Then, on the lower right of the design, use the arrow button to shrink the icons to suit an ornament. Ornaments of Wood slice are averaged 2.5-3″ in diameter, so you should stay inside that size.

When you've scaled it, make sure to press the connect button in the layers menu's bottom right corner to ensure that the template is cut precisely as it seems to you. Or Else, Cricut would want to cram all into as little room as possible. You're now going to press the 'make it' icon.

When you've arrived at the screen of the mat, press on the designs and drag them apart a little. Since we're producing stencils, they won't fit if they're too near together.

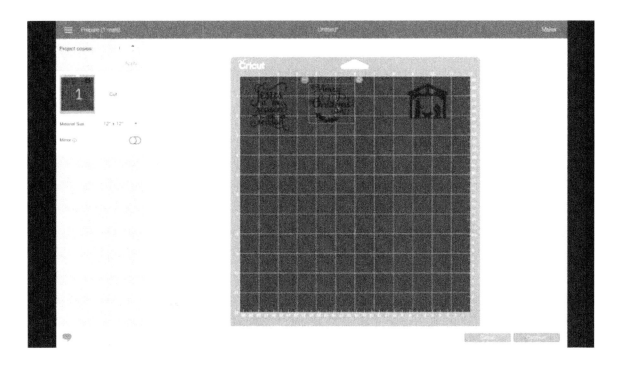

The designs were cut on Oracle Stencil Film, which can be purchased directly from Amazon.

You'll eradicate the center and abandon the outer portions of the vinyl while producing stencils. Weeding labels or jersey patterns is the inverse of this.

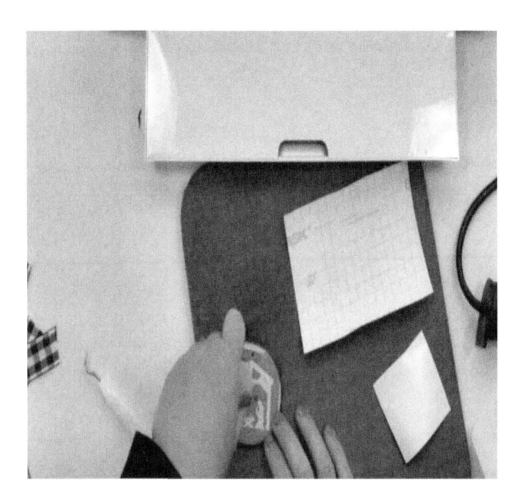

Step 2: Transferring the Stencil

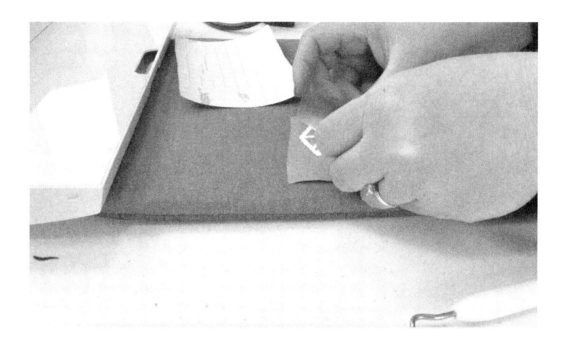

Place the transfer paper onto the Stencil so you can shift it to the ornaments of wood slice after all of the parts have been weeded out. Use plain contact paper for transfer tape, which can be found in most stores such as Walmart.

Smoothly move the paper down with the scraper tool to ensure it adheres to all the vinyl.

Get rid of the backing from the vinyl stencil and put it on the wood-slice decoration. Take all the time you need aligning the Stencil; as far as you don't press it flat, you'll be free to pass it around to the middle.

Using the scraper tool to stick the Stencil to the wood slice until you've got the design centered. Take the transition document away from you gently now. Be certain that all of the stencil bits adhere to the wood.

For any bits, try to unstick with the transfer tape; simply re-scrape and set it down again.

Use the scorch marker until all of the stencils are in place.

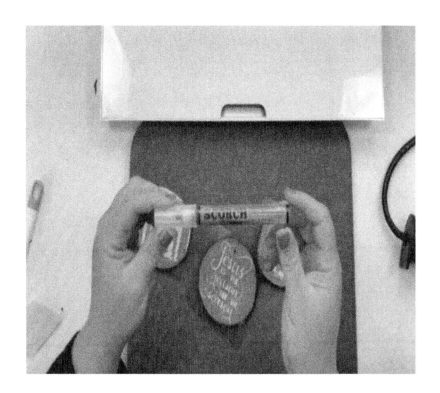

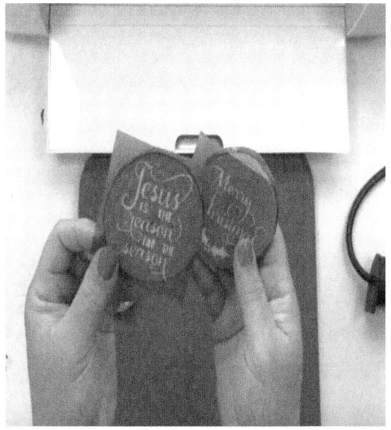

Step 3: Filling the Stencil with the Scorch Marker

When using the scorch marker for the first time, give it a good shake. And take a scrap of paper and use it in priming the marker. You can choose to include the backs of your ornaments.

However, you'll need a place to repeatedly force down the marker's tip. It can take a long time to prime the market for the first time. Continue until the liquid comes out of the marker's edge.

Start to fill in all open areas of the Stencil with the marker after it has been prepared.

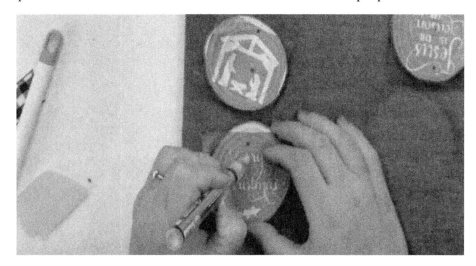

If the marker is well primed, the wood can shift color almost automatically. You might need to again prime the marker when you go if you're making a tonne of ornaments. Strip the wood slice ornament with stencils until you've finished coloring on all of the ornaments with the scorch pen.

You might need to use your weeding method to remove the stencil pieces. You can also check where you used the marker.

You can use a heat gun now to really get it out.

Step 4: Using a Heat Gun, apply heat

For a moment, let's talk of the heat gun. This stuff gets wet, hot enough to bubble in the finishing off the table. Heat up the silicone chairs.

You can use a heat shield pad to cover your table if you do this. You can also use the same heat pressing mat you used for tops.

Adjust the heat gun to low or medium-high and switch it about as you would a hairdryer while drying your hair.

You'll see the picture darkening when the wood-slice ornaments heat up. It can take a few minutes after adding heat to show the full effect.

Allow the ornaments to cool before handling them. They'll be nice and cozy.

Step 5: Use Mod Podge or another sealant to seal the project.

I'm not sure if the sealer's purpose is to shield your ornament or to pop the wood-burned image. It makes a huge improvement in the appearance of your ornament.

So don't forget to use the sealer. Applying Mod Podge to the surface will perform the job perfectly.

Step 6: Add Bows and Ribbons

Attach a string or a bit of twine to mount the decoration once the sealer has dried. And, to top it off, you can hot glued on bows or any other embellishments you like.

You can create your own forms of the Hulk, Captain America, Batman, Spiderman, Ironman, and Donatello, the Ninja Turtle, after scouring the Cricut Design Space Library for all the required design elements. These masks are simple to put on and take off, and they cover enough of the face!

These DIY Superhero Masks came together quickly and easily thanks to a few factors. First, use your Cricut Maker to cut out all of the various bits, so you don't have to do all of the careful cutting with your hand. Second, use Cricut's brand new Easy Press Mini to put them together, which made adding all the tiny information a breeze!

The Cricut Easy Press Mini

Cricut's Easy Press Mini is the latest member of the Easy Press family. It has the same heat plate and dries as the larger heat presses, but it's much smaller and has a precision top. It has 3 separate heat levels and a heat-proof foundation and measures just 3.4 x 2.1″. It's lightweight, simple to use, and perfect for small,

informative projects!

When you should use a larger heat press to add these little iron-on specifics, the EasyPress Mini can help you to operate in tight spaces, ensuring that each tiny part was completely stable. The Mini is also great for circular things (like hats, shoes, bows) and patterns in or near seams and pockets, in addition to minor cuts like the ones used here.

One of the favorite aspects of occupied with the Easy Press Mini is how much smoother layering iron-on bits is! Instead of trying to shield the lowest layers from contact with a bigger heat press or overheating previous layers, the Easy Press Mini can help you to get into tiny spaces and heat just the parts that you

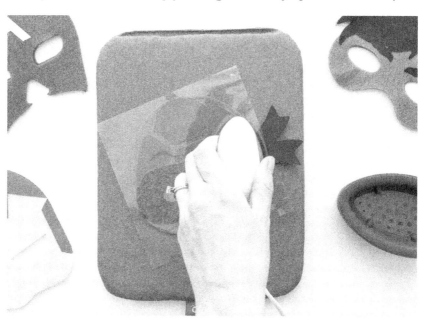

want!

Supplies Needed

These masks are incredibly easy to create and take just minutes to put together. Here's what you'll require:

- Cricut Maker

- Easy Press Mini

- Hot Glue Gun

- Easy Press Mat

- Iron-On Vinyl

- Felt

- Fold-Over Elastic

SUPPLIES NEEDED:
FELT
IRON-ON
5/8" FOLD OVER ELASTIC

TOOLS NEEDED:
CRICUT MACHINE
CRICUT EASYPRESS MINI
EASYPRESS MAT
HOT GLUE GUN

Cutting Out Mask Pieces

Many of the "decorative" features are crafted from iron-on vinyl and fixed to the front of the masks, which are made up of 2 layers of felt fused together. You'll need to use a Cricut machine to cut out all of the parts until you've built and measured your masks to suit your girl.

Begin by cutting out two felt mask bases for each mask you're creating. When you use the Cricut Maker's Rotary Blade, you'll get perfect cuts from the felt!

Then, using iron-on vinyl, cut out all of the mask specifics. Make sure the "Mirror" button on the cut screen is chosen, and then pick out all the bad aspects of the logo until they can be attached to the masks.

1.3 Iron On Mask Details

You'll want to apply all of the iron-on information to the upper layer before mounting the masks. You'll want to link to the cooperating Cricut Easy Press Heat Guide while operating with every Cricut EasyPress to ensure you're using the correct settings. It urges you to set your EasyPress Mini to the Low setting by

choosing the Easy Press

Mini, felt as the base coat, and iron-on as the heat-transfer content. The felt mask should be Pre-heat for around 5 seconds until the EasyPress Mini is hot.

Then, iron the iron-on information on topmost of the mask for around 30 seconds while rotating the Easy Press Mini with a gentle touch. Remove the transparent transfer layer until iron-on materials and the mask have properly cooled. Continue to apply iron-on detailing to the front mask before it is over.

Assembling The Mask

Once you've finished the front mask, it's time to put it together! Place the two mask bits, right sides down, onto your work surface.

Begin by applying a very narrow line of hot glue to the opposite side of the lower layer over one eye. Until the adhesive sets, lock the top sheet, right-side-up, to ensure that the eye holes are correctly aligned. Rep on the opposite eye.

Safe the elastic after the eyes have been taped shut. On one line, glue one corner of the fold-over elastic to one side and then the other. Check that the elastic is not bent and that it is long enough to go around your

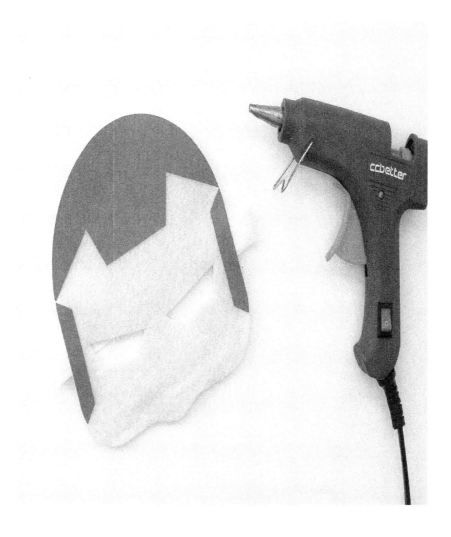

child's head.

NOTE: Start with at least 11 inches of elastic and incorporate more if required!

The final move is to join the 2 layers across the edge with adhesive. The mask layers would tend to be one continuous piece until finished if the glue line is kept quite thin and near to the ground!

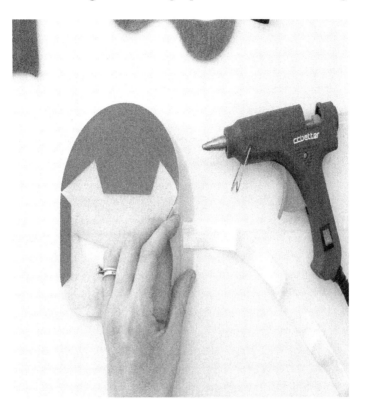

After you've finished one mask, repeat with as many superheroes as you like! Then make a few more because they're so simple and enjoyable!

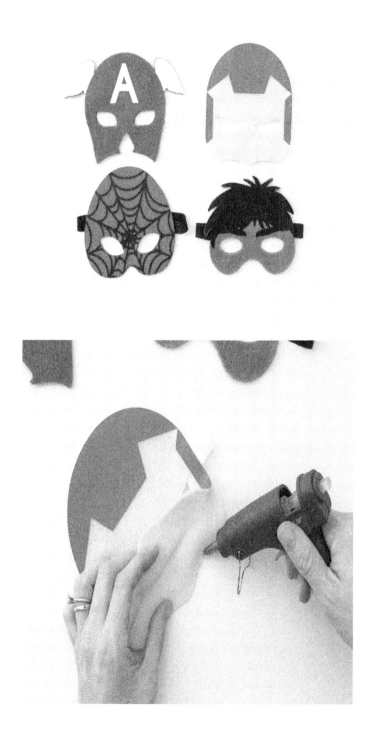

Finally, give them to the children and let their dreams run wild!

While you have the time of dressing all year in your homes, these masks will make perfect Halloween costumes. These are perfect for little children and babies that don't want anything on their appearances because of their tiny size, fluffy felt, and stretchy elastic. If you're short of time, their easy-and-quick assembly can help you throw together costumes in no time (particularly if you match the masks with these twenty-minute capes!).

These DIY Superhero Masks are a lot of fun to create, and using the Cricut Easy Press Mini eliminates a great deal of the frustration that comes with iron-on creations. If you create them for Halloween or just for fun, they'll be worth your time and will guarantee big ol' smiles on your kids' faces!

DO-IT-YOURSELF

SUPER HERO MASKS
WITH THE CRICUT EASYPRESS MINI

Chapter 2: Cricut Project Ideas III

There are about as many Cricut ideas as there are humans, multiplied by the materials available. You can make great DIY crafts for every purpose with a Cricut Maker, Cricut Explore, or the adorable Cricut Joy.

Let's have a look at several projects that range from simple to difficult.

2.1. Tassels

Tassels may be used in a variety of ways. These are extremely simple to produce and can be made to fit any task. Use them as a keyring or zipper pick, add them to the sides of pillows or covers, hang them from a rope to create a banner, and a thousand other items! You may even make them out of leather or faux leather for a more elegant look. Tassels look great on almost everything.

Materials

- Fabric mat

- 12" x 18" fabric rectangles

- Glue gun

- Cricut machine

Instructions

- Launch Design Space to begin a new design.

- Click the "Image" icon in the bottom left-hand corner and type "tassel" into the search box.

- Press "Insert" after selecting the illustration of a rectangle with lines on either side.

- Arrange fabric on the mat and use the Cricut to cut out the pattern.

- Take the fabric off the mat and save the excess square.

- Beginning from the uncut side, position the material face down and roll tightly. As required, untangle the fringe.

- To attach the tassel at the top, use some waste fabric and a hot glue stick.

- Use your beautiful tassels to decorate anything you like!

2.2. Paw Print Socks

Socks are the epitome of comfort. Small paw prints add a cool, secret decoration to the base of your socks. Every time you cuddle up, show off your affection towards pets. You can do this with about every small style or even add text to the base of your foot to add a quotation. You can select any kind of socks you choose. Please ensure the sock and vinyl colors contrast for easy reading. Or, for a hidden design, make them all in the same color! Under certain lighting, the vinyl shine will contrast with the fabric. You'll require your Cricut EasyPress or iron for this since it uses heat transfer vinyl.

Materials

- Socks

- Weeding tool or pick

- Scrap cardboard

- Heat transfer vinyl

- Cutting mat

- Cricut EasyPress or iron

- Cricut machine

Instructions

- Build a new project in Cricut Design Space.

- Check for "paw prints" using the "Photo" button in the bottom left-hand corner.

- Select your preferred paw prints and click "Insert."

- Send the pattern to the Cricut by placing the iron-on material on the mat.

- To eliminate excess material, use a pick or weeding tool.

- Take the material from the mat and stuff the socks with scrap cardboard.

- Put the iron-on material onto the socks' bottoms.

- To attach it to the iron-on material, use EasyPress.

- Take the cardboard from the socks after they have cooled.

- Put on your adorable paw print socks!

2.3. Monogrammed Drawstring Bag

Drawstring bags are simple to use and carry. They're just as easy to produce as they are to use! These bags can be kept on hand for anyone in your family to pick and go as required. You may use monograms to distinguish them, or you can use a different pattern on each one to modify it for a certain purpose or simply to decorate it. This can also be used as gift bags! The designs are made of heat transfer vinyl, so you'll need your Cricut EasyPress or iron for this project.

Materials

- Heat transfer vinyl

- Two matching rectangles of fabric

- Weeding tool or pick

- Cutting mat

- Needle and thread

- Ribbon

- Cricut machine

- Cricut EasyPress or iron

Instructions

- Build a new project in Cricut Design Space.

- Check for "monogram" using the "Image" icon in the bottom left-hand corner.

- Select the monogram you want to use and press "Insert."

- Place the shiny liner side of the iron-on material on the mat and give the pattern to the Cricut.

- To eliminate excess material, use the weeding tool or a pick.

- Remove the monogram out of the mat.

- The monogram should be centered on your material and moved down a couple of inches, so it doesn't get rolled up as the ribbon is created.

- The pattern should be ironed onto the fabric.

- Put the two rectangles along such that the fabric's outside side is faced inward.

- Leave a seam allowance when you sew along with the corners. Let the top open and stop it a few inches below the top.

- Fold the bag's top back until the stitches are reached.

- Sew around the folded edge's bottom, keeping the sides open.

- Turn bag's right side out.

- The ribbon should be threaded through the loop at the top of the bag.

- Bring what you need in your fresh drawstring pocket!

2.4. Customized Pillow

A simple concept that is often requested and quick to personalize. Make the pillow of your dreams!

Materials

- Insert Cricut Access

- Protective Sheet Pillow Cover

- Glitter Iron-On Vinyl

- Iron-On

- Cricut Easypress Mat

- Cricut Machine

Instructions

- From the Home tab of the Cricut Design Space, select "New Project."

- Click the text icon in the lower right corner of the page and choose the font you like. Fill in your name and adjust the size of the box corner to fit your pillow.

- To add an additional bit of text for your Est. Year, choose the Text button. Drag and arrange your last name properly.

- Choose all textboxes at the same time and hit the attach button. It will link the two text boxes, allowing for precise cutting.

- The screen appears as you click the "Make It" icon. Allow that the Mirror is turned on.

- To switch on and off the mirror setting, click the image in the upper left corner. The image above appears on the computer. Turn the "off" switch on.

- Press the Mirror button; the mat will now reflect your mirrored image, and you're ready to load your Iron-On Vinyl shiny side down onto your mat. Follow the instructions by clicking and dragging.

- Weed the excess vinyl and center the pillow cover design once the design has been sliced.

- Use the Easypress Settings Chart to set the timer and temperature for your material.

- Use the Iron-On Protection Sheet to cover the structure, then top it with the Easypress and press the Cricut button. When it has beeped, remove it. Heat for 10 to 15 seconds on the other side of your pillow cover.

- Enable the iron-on to cool before removing the sheet.

2.5. Cricut Gift Boxes

What is the point of creating crafts if you don't gift them? You may even create your own box designs after you've become more comfortable with the Design Space software – nothing beats training for honing a talent. Let's have a look at how you should get started designing your own gift boxes right now.

Materials

- Scoring wheel

- Cardstock (Glitter or of your choice)

- Glue

- Cricut machine

Instructions

- Launch Cricut Design Space and choose "New Project," then import the SVG file patterns you've searched or downloaded. Alternately, start creating your own box patterns.

- Start with the pillowcase package, which is probably the easiest to create for a novice. Using the upper formatting panel in Design Space, resize the patterns to suit the box's expected size. If you're producing more than one box, make sure to click "Ungroup" to distinguish the prototypes that need to be cut and assembled separately. Before submitting the design to cutting, make sure to adjust the Line form to "Score" for any sections of the model that should be folded. After you've finished scoring the lines which have to be folded, pick the whole pattern and click on "Attach," then finish sizing, if necessary, before clicking "Make it."

- When deciding on cutting settings under "Make it," use cardstock as your chosen material. You should start cutting after you've arranged the material and the cutting pad.

- Assemble the box(es) you'll be using. You won't need to use adhesive to hold the pieces of the box intact if you use light materials like paper or standard cardstock. If you're using glitter cardstock or similar materials, though, you'll need to glue all of the pieces of the package together except the portion that's meant to seal it.

- Begin putting together your package, gluing the pieces that need to be sealed while you move. To help it go smoother and more efficiently, use tacky glue or a glue gun. And your box is all set!

2.6. Personalized Christmas Ornaments

Materials

- Heat-Resistant Tape

- Cardstock (white)

- Sublimation Ornaments in Blank Form

- Butcher paper

- Mat and EasyPress 2

- Explore Air 2 Machine or Cricut Maker

- Buffalo Check Cricut Infusible Ink Transfer Sheet

- Cloth without any lint

Instructions

- Create your own personalized holiday ornaments by starting a new design in Cricut Design Space.

- For the front and back of each ornament, place two 2.81" circles. Using the slice feature to generate negative space photographs of the designs within the circle after adding your favorite holiday photos and custom text to the circle.

- Cut your designs with your Cricut machine (ensure to mirror your picture before cutting!) and weed the unwanted Infusible Ink with your fingertips or tweezers.

- Remove any dust, dirt, or smudges from the ornament's surface with a lint-free fabric.

- Apply Infusible Ink on both sections of the blank ornament and cover with heat-resistant tape.

- Preheat the EasyPress 2 to 400°F and set the timer for 240 seconds. Cover with another layer of butcher paper after placing the ornaments on top of the butcher paper.

- Place the EasyPress 2 on top of the decorations for 240 seconds; just don't press down! Place the EasyPress 2 back on its base after the loop is over, then carefully peel the top layer of butcher paper.

2.7 Christmas Tea Towels

Christmas tea towels are a simple and quick way to get started with the Cricut cutting unit. Simply use heat transfer vinyl to provide almost limitless design options.

Materials

- Tea towel with a deer silhouette

- Tea towel "Merry and Bright."

- flour sack towels (white)

- Cut files and iron-on for Christmas tea towels.

- Tool for weeding

- press cloth or parchment paper.

- Iron or EasyPress

- Cricut Explore Air 2 or Cricut Maker

Instructions

- In Design Space, open the Christmas tea towel cut file(s).

- Adjust the sizes and colors to your liking. Don't neglect to mirror the text while cutting the iron-on vinyl for your Christmas tea towels.

- Choose the materials. The cutting material on the Cricut Maker is selected directly in Design Space; many of the most popular cutting material choices may appear.

- With the weeder unit, remove any negative space from the designs.

- Place the patterns on the towel with the liners and see where you like them.

- Set the EasyPress's temperature and timer according to the instructions for the material you're ironing on and the material you're ironing on to. Preheat the tea towel by ironing it to prevent any wrinkles. Cover the pattern with the press cloth or parchment paper and press down tightly for the period shown on the map. To begin the timer, press the right-hand Cricut button. Enable the liners to cool down for a moment after the timer goes off before trying to peel them off.

Replace the filler and click for another 5–10 seconds if some aspect of the pattern starts to pull up.

Chapter 3: Tips And Trick

Using a Cricut is a thrilling experience. For a novice, it may even be intimidating and daunting. These 28 Cricut Tricks and Secrets can save your sanity and help you remain more organized along the way, whether you're a newcomer or a professional Cricut crafter.

3.1 Cricut Tricks and Secrets

1. Peel the mat instead of material

While it can sound natural to peel the material (vinyl, cardstock, etc.) away from the surface, it is simply preferable to softly curl and peel the mat away from the stuff. This helps to save the art supplies from being so distorted.

2. For vinyl storage, use IKEA plastic bags.

IKEA plastic bag storage holders are another favorite Cricut hacks that have gained some attention in recent years. They're great for keeping vinyl rolls. You can even get some on the internet!

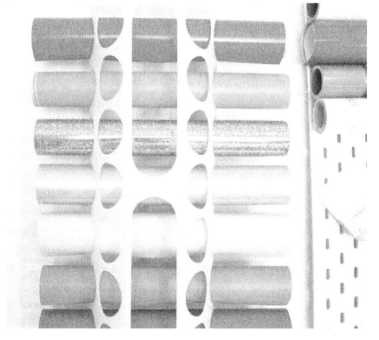

3. Tin foil should be used to sharpen the razor.

Sharpening the fine-point blade with tin foil will quickly prolong its life! In reality, using tin foil will extend the blade's life by three times! Remove the blade from the clamp and pass the edge 10-12 times through the tin foil with the blade to sharpen it.

4. keep your knives in the Cricut.

This could seem self-evident, but as a novice Cricut user, you may have no idea that the interior of your system could store the blades and small tools in a dust-free, secure manner.

5. Pick up little fragments from your pad or pattern with a lint roller (Works for glitter too)

You should quickly catch the excess little bits on a lint roller if you have an elaborate pattern cut out on paper or vinyl to save time!

It's still great for picking up stray glitter on your desk.

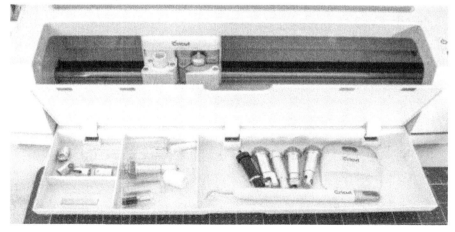

6. In spite of using Cricut pens for your laptop, use pen adapters.

The ability to have your Cricut machine compose for you is a fantastic function. You'll actually wish you could use pens rather than Cricut pens at some stage.

The good news is that if you have an Explore 2 or later, you can buy pen adapters that will enable you to use almost any brand of a pen! Sharpies, brush pens, and more are all available!

How to Use ALL these Pens with Your Cricut!

1. Sharpie Fine Point
2. Sharpie Ultra Fine Point
3. Sharpie Pen Art Pen
4. Pilot Precise
5. Bic Marking
6. Bic Cristal
7. Sakura Gelly Roll
8. Amaza Gel Pens
9. Sharpie Oil-Based Paint
10. Uni-ball Signo UM-153
11. Crayola Fine Line Marker
12. Crayola Super Tip
13. Crayola Detailing Gel Pen
14. Tombow Duel Brush Pens

7. For vinyl remnants, use a nail polish tray.

One of most favorite Cricut hacks is this one! When weeding, get a cheap nail polish holder to catch tiny

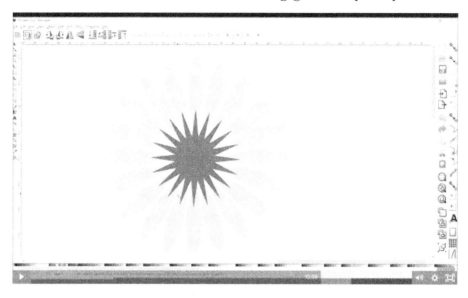

vinyl bits.

8. Inkscape is a free program that allows you to create your own SVG cut files.

SVG files for Design Space can be found for free or purchased by Cricut Access. So what if you had your own? After all, there are occasions when there is a need to introduce a specific vision to life or customize an object. Inkscape is a free, open-source software for creating SVG files from nothing or converting images to layered SVG files.

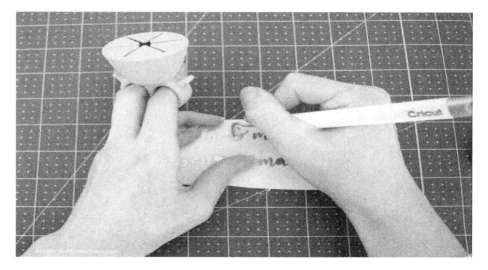

9. Converting a picture to an SVG is as simple as clicking a button

If you aren't ready to learn how to build your own SVG files, use the one-click picture to SVG converter instead.

10. Use a pegboard to keep all of your Cricut materials organized

Pegboards are vital for keeping supplies ordered, and you can save money by using unused wall space! These can be used at Amazon or on IKEA. Plus, Cricut hacks like this really help to make your craft room look nice.

11. Baby wipes may be used to clean your mat. Resticky the mat with Easy Tack

Cleaning the dirt off of recycled Cricut mats with baby wipes will give them a new lease on existence. You may even re-sticky every mat for another 5-10 uses by spraying it with a few coats of Easy Tack.

12. To hold vinyl rolls tight, use slap bracelets.

If you have a lot of vinyl, then keep the rolls in a variety of places. Slap bracelets are an inexpensive way to keep vinyl rolls intact.

13. Sort the vinyl into wood bins by type.

It's important to keep track of your vinyl styles (iron-on, textured, adhesive, etc.). Bins may be a convenient way to organize items by category and mark each bin for easy identification.

14. Trim vinyl with a smooth edge to prevent rough corners.

If you're not patient, vinyl is one of the materials that can easily be thrown away. Trimming the vinyl before cutting can help hold the edges straight and reduce waste.

15. Discover fantastic SVG freebies

Free SVG files for Design Space can be listed on Pinterest searches, among other sites. There is a huge Freebie Vault at Abbi Kirsten Collections of over 150 free SVG and printable models!

16. For tougher fabrics, use painter's tape

Painters tape will be your best buddy if your things are rolling around on your mat. It's particularly relevant when working with wood and chipboard.

17. When adding vinyl to angled surfaces, cut slits in the transfer tape.

On a curved wall, how can you get the vinyl to be smooth?

Aside from practice, one technique is to make slits along the edges of the transfer tape. This gives the tape some wiggle room when you position the pattern.

18. Use cheat sheets to help you remember what each feature does.

Understanding Cricut terminology and the features in Design Space may be difficult to remember; a glossary cheat sheet may be very useful. You can also get it online.

19. Use a magazine holder to store vinyl remnants.

Don't throw out the odd and ends of vinyl! Small cuts can also be made for them. To see what you have to deal from, keep your scraps in a plain magazine holder.

20. Make use of a printable environment guide

Trying to recall any of those content settings or custom settings, much as Design Space features is almost difficult! There is a free guide on the subject that you can find inside the Freebie Vault!

21. On wood, use iron-on vinyl (HTV).

Well, indeed! Iron-on vinyl should be used on wood! To make it easier, Cricut has heat guidance. The look of heat transfer vinyl to that of adhesive vinyl is preferred mostly.

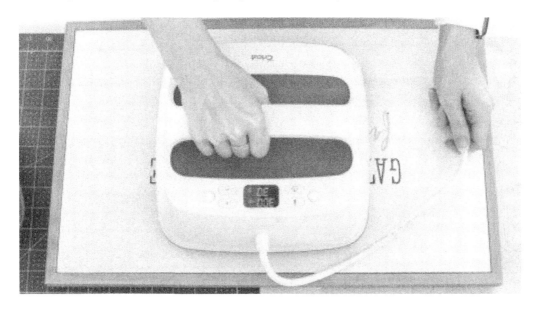

22. Use the Cricut Easy Mini-Press to apply iron-on vinyl to tumblers.

In 2019, Cricut launched the Easypress Micro, a miniature variant of the Easypress. This little gadget is so adorable and useful that it also allows you to iron on vinyl to your tumblers!

23. Freebies can be found in the Cricut Design Room.

Did you realize that every week, Cricut releases a new package of freebies that anybody can use, even if they don't have Cricut Access?! Freebies can be found under Images > Filter > Freebies!

24. Understand where to look for the right fabrics

It can take a long time and a lot of trial and error to figure out where to find the best-priced Cricut products. You can take help from the internet regarding this.

25. Use the internet to find free fonts.

You're losing out if you haven't yet mastered the strength of downloading free fonts for your Cricut. Check out the internet for the top 60 free and paid fonts, as well as exclusive Christmas font posts!

26. Import specialty projects to build a room using character maps

It's one thing to download fonts, but it's quite another to learn how to make a word appear like a million bucks! It took me a while to figure out that you can navigate those unique scrolly letters using your computer's "character charts" or "glyphs."

1. Go to your PC's "search" function and look for "character map" or "character viewer" on the Mac.
2. Pick your preferred font from the drop-down menu.
3. Scroll down before you reach the letter you're looking for.
4. Pick it with a click, then copy it.
5. In Design Space, paste the font character into the text box.

27. Maintain a list of your favorite vinyl records.

There is so much vinyl that it's difficult to keep track of them all! There are several styles, textures, and labels of vinyl to keep track of. To keep track, keep pieces of vinyl on a metal ring labeled with the brand and form of vinyl so you can still locate your favorite vinyl!

28. Keep supplies and machines in storage carts.

It's important to keep the supplies and machinery secure. A storage rolling cart is one of the favorite ways to do this! Check out your nearest Michaels shop!

3.2 Mat Maintenance and Longevity

Since the mats are costly, you will want to retain them in service for a long time. The best way to extend the existence of a mat is to treat it carefully and properly. Here are some tips about how to take control of these mats:

- After each use, replace the transparent cover/film on the sheet. Which will keep the mat clean and free of dirt and dust.
- Use a lint roller to remove any substance debris from the mat surface during each use.
- Use non-alcoholic wipes to clean the mat.
- Wash the mats with soapy water, except for the silk mat. The cotton mat is unlike any other mat in that it cannot be washed with water.
- Using a scraper, clean any object debris from the mat surface except the cloth mat.

3.3 Cricut Maker Specialty Equipment

Aside from the blades, there are other specialized instruments for purposes other than cutting.

Markers and pens

There is a space for markers and pens next to the blade housing. If you want to design greeting cards and want to use elegant fonts, this is the place to go. The Cricut is compatible with a wide range of pens and markers. Markers and pens must be purchased separately.

Scoring Wheel

This is a one-of-a-kind feature. This scoring wheel is your buddy if you don't need to cut a pattern but only need to fold a piece of material. This feature can be used for a variety of things, like creating personalized crates and making a Greeting card.

Single and double scoring tips are the two forms of scoring tips available. Depending on the project, you will use the same housing with all styles of tips.

Fast Swap Housing and Helpful Tips

This is sole housing that can be used for a variety of feature tips. The tips that can be used colloquially with this housing are explained in the following section.

Foil Transfer Tip

This is one of the most recent Cricut Maker functions. This is used to embellish and bling up the finished products. It's designed to be used with foil covers.

Deboss tip

This tip is similar to the engraving tip, but it is designed for finer, lighter materials. Foil, dense card paper, and basswood may all be decorated with it.

Engrave tip

This tip may be used to engrave texts or monograms on a variety of items. Plastic mats, leather and metal sheets are the best materials for this. With this tip, you will make the projects more special.

Perforation Tip

Tear-off materials are often used for a project. The perforation tip is used for this reason. This tip works well for lightweight fabrics.

Wavy tip

This tip can come in handy when creating greeting cards. This results in wavy edges, which provide a decorative touch. It may be used to embellish card corners, as well as iron-on vinyl and other textured sheets.

Conclusion

Thank you for making it to the end. While you're reading this, it's reasonable to conclude with the various project information included in this book; you are ready to create new project ideas.

Crafting is fun, love, hobby and the best use of leisure time. But sometimes, it becomes hard and frustrating. For this, Cricut brings remarkable technology accompanied by so many machines, design software, materials, tools and accessories to make your design come true.

This guidebook was created to help you understand the potential of your Cricut device in terms of the designs it can create. Using a Cricut should be incredibly easy for you at this stage, and one of the main reasons that people prefer Cricut to do their cutting is that they are easy to use. If you have the proper tools, it's simple to use and understand. Since it is not overly complex, almost everyone can set a Cricut unit. What a potential customer has to do is obey the simple guidelines that arrive with the package.

So, you've mastered Cricut Design Space; you're a master crafter, what now? Why don't you bring your skills to good use? Now that you've seen a few examples of projects which can be done with a Cricut, you may have a few more ideas about how to utilize your latest gadget.

But bear in mind that you can never quit researching, attempting new ideas, or becoming imaginative. The Cricut does not make you any less innovative; it just simplifies the method such that you can devote your precious time and energy to more critical tasks, such as personalizing the ideas after they've been cut. It takes the boring work off your hands and turns it into something enjoyable, easy, and fast. Make your life, your house, and the homes of your companions more entertaining and built by using this!

Last but not least, keep in mind! You don't have to be a professional or an expert at making stuff. Give the Cricut a try to do the hard work for you, and you'll be pleased with the results.

I hope you've gained a lot of knowledge.

Printed in Great Britain
by Amazon